SURVIVING THE UNEXPECTED

Fall safety training for horse riders

Lindsay Nylund

Copyright © Lindsay Nylund 2015

Illustrations by: Natasha Jackson

Cover Photo: Joe McInally Photography
Rider: Sofia Holmgren

Demonstration of Techniques: Riley Nylund

All rights reserved. This book or any portion thereof shall not be copied, reproduced, lent, resold, hired out, or otherwise circulated in any manner without the express written permission of the copyright owner except for the use of brief quotations in a book review, media report, industry news or scholarly journal.

First Printing: 2016

ISBN 978-0-9946397-3-8 (hardback)
ISBN 978-0-9946397-0-7 (paperback)
ISBN 978-0-9946397-1-4 (mobi)
ISBN 978-0-9946397-2-1 (epub)

Enquiries about fall safety training, consultation requests, video analysis of fall incidents, instructor accreditation programs, and training program design can be made via:

email: horseriderfallsafety@gmail.com
web: www.horseriderfallsafety.com

Feedback and suggestions for improvement to future editions welcome.

DISCLAIMER: Due to the high-risk nature of horse riding activity, the risk of serious injury or death cannot be eliminated by safety measures and the information and techniques detailed in this book. Participation in any physical activity including horse rider fall safety training involves risk of injury. To minimise these risks do not do training beyond your level of aptitude, fitness or confidence; consult a medical practitioner if you have any limitations or are recovering from injury; and learn under the supervision of a qualified instructor as recommended in this book.

To my family and to all horse riders.

I would also like to remember my gymnastics teacher, Akos Kovacs. Had Akos not jumped, handcuffed, from a moving train to escape a labour camp in 1948, and held on tightly to his tuck position, this book would never have been written.

CONTENTS

FOREWORD — vii
PREFACE — viii
ACKNOWLEDGEMENTS — x

INTRODUCTION

History — 1
Research and Studies — 2
Dispelling Some Myths — 5
Safety Considerations — 9
Rider Self-help Guide: How to Use This Book — 11
Fall Safety Instructor Guide: How to Use This Book — 13

THEORY AND SCIENCE

Fall and Response Times — 15
Spontaneity and Unconscious Learning — 23
Emergency Dismount — 25
Fall Scenarios and Fall Safety Skills — 28
Biomechanics and Forces of Impact — 37
Simulation, Skills Transfer, and Retention — 43
Fall Safety Technique Analysis — 49

SKILL LEARNING AND TRAINING METHODS

Warm-up and Conditioning Exercises — 53
Body Shapes and Basic Positions — 62
Basic Rolling and Tumbling Skills — 69
Basic Aerial Skills — 78
Height, Landing Surface, and Speed Progression — 86
Dive Roll Drills and Skills — 98
Forward Somersault — 108

VAULTING SKILLS AND SIMULATION ACTIVITIES

Vaulting Skills — 117
Fall Simulation Activities — 124
Pre-ride Safety Routines — 141

SKILLS ASSESSMENT — 152
REFERENCES — 157
INDEX — 160
ABOUT THE AUTHOR — 163

FOREWORD

I have known Lindsay Nylund from his successful gymnastics career where he represented Australia at the World Championships and the Olympic and Commonwealth Games. His dedication, drive, talent and knowledge elevated him to the pinnacle of gymnastics, winning the first ever international medal in gymnastics for Australia—a silver medal in the men's all-around competition at the 1978 Commonwealth Games in Edmonton, Canada. As national coach at the time, I had the pleasure to be coach of this team, which won a bronze medal. Many years have passed since that historic time for gymnastics in Australia and, after meeting recently, I was not surprised to see him taking on this current challenge.

Lindsay's knowledge and technical expertise, thorough approach to training, and compelling logic can provide incredible safety benefits to horse riders. This book and the system of training includes a review of research and is based on sound scientific principles and training methods. The feedback I have seen from training sessions gives me great confidence that it will equip riders with life-saving skills that can significantly reduce the risk of catastrophic injury should they fall from their horse.

I commend this book and the acceptance of the need to undertake fall safety training to all riders, and to organisations and individuals who are responsible for rider safety. Every rider who learns the skills will be empowered to feel safer, be far better prepared, and minimise their risk of serious injury in a fall.

Barry Cheales

Olympic Gymnast
Former National Coach
Order of Australia Medal

From 2008 to 2013, I was National Medical Officer for the Australian Racing Board and during this time I was awarded a Winston Churchill Fellowship to study improvements in international health protection standards for jockeys in the UK, Ireland, France and Germany, and recommend improvements to Australian standards. More can be done to improve jockey and rider health and safety and this includes learning fall safety skills. As an injury countermeasure, fall safety training is being taken seriously in a number of the countries that I visited. It is a known industry problem that the majority of injuries are a result of riders falling from their horse.

It is wonderful that Lindsay has crystallised the training methods and skills in this book, which provides a practical and effective solution to reduce injury risk. Riders who learn these skills from a young age—in particular pony club riders, those doing higher risk equestrian activities such as jumps, and apprentice jockeys—can benefit significantly from the training and the associated muscle memory. I recommend this book to all horse riders and industry professionals.

Dr Caron Jander   MBBCh, MPhil (Sports Med), FAFOEM, FACSM, FACAsM

Consultant Occupational Physician
Former National Medical Officer, Australian Racing Board

PREFACE

Falls, in which riders have had their lives or careers tragically cut short, prompted me to analyse some videos of how riders respond when falling. After more than twenty years experience as a former Olympic gymnast and coach of gymnasts from beginner to international level, I was very concerned with what I saw. Most riders have not been trained in fall safety skills! This was a call to action for me—something needed to be done about this.

Because of the nature of horse riding activity, most people who ride regularly will fall from their horse at some point. Riders who participate in higher-risk activities such as racing, track-work, cross-country and other equestrian activities that involve jumps, polo, and rodeo are likely to fall from their horse on many occasions.

My review of research in the area of jockey and equestrian safety, along with consultation with industry professionals, made it clear to me that little has been done to implement proper fall safety training for riders on a systematic and industry-wide basis. In addition to reducing the risks of catastrophic and serious injury, fall safety training can improve injury outcomes of a less serious nature, such as broken collarbones and arm, leg and soft-tissue injuries.

The skills and training methods detailed in this book are based on gymnastics techniques—modified to maximise safety in fall incidents. The Introduction and Theory and Science sections are designed to improve knowledge and understanding and are relevant for riders, riding instructors, fall safety instructors and industry professionals. There are a number of basic activities and skills that can be practiced using this book as a self-help guide, and other skills and activities that need to be learned under the supervision and instruction of a qualified fall safety instructor. The skills and activities that can be learned and practiced unsupervised are summarised in the introductory section 'Rider Self-help Guide: How to Use This Book'.

It behoves governing bodies, industry administrators, committees and individuals responsible for rider safety to implement policies that provide proper fall safety training to riders of all disciplines. The cost of training is likely to be substantially less than the cost of support and rehabilitation for riders who suffer injuries that can be prevented or mitigated. No sum of money can make up for loss of life. We owe it to these courageous athletes and riders from all disciplines to protect them in every way possible so they can pursue their profession, their sport or their hobby with a higher degree of safety. I hope this book will be a catalyst for change, and that riders of all ages and disciplines will accept the need to be educated and trained in fall safety skills that are appropriate for their age, ability and horse riding activity.

Lindsay Nylund

Facing your fears

A ten year old gymnast I was coaching for the Junior Elite National Championships inexplicably developed a fear that stopped her from performing one of the compulsory skills: a back-flip on the 10 centimetre-wide balance beam.

After much discussion and going back through all of the basics, she eventually confessed that she had recently had a frighteningly vivid nightmare in which her hands missed the beam when performing the back-flip and she hit her head on the beam. The frightening image from her nightmare could not be dispelled by conscious reasoning or by getting her to focus on the correct movement sequence.

I concluded that the only way for her to conquer her fear was to face it head-on by consciously allowing the image to appear in her mind as she was about to jump backward, and then continue into the back-flip regardless. The strategy was to change the *unexpected* to the *expected* and free her unconscious mind to perform the back-flip as she had successfully done many times before. Though amused by this strategy, she agreed to follow this advice.

After a few attempts at doing the back-flip with assistance, and allowing the frightening image to be part of the movement sequence, she once again began to perform the back-flip on the high beam. She had faced her fear and the image that had found its way into her thought process soon disappeared completely.

Three weeks later she won the Junior National Championships and was selected for the Junior-Elite National Gymnastics squad.

Riders who accept that they are likely to fall from their horse can learn to actively respond and reduce their risk of injury in a fall. Riders who do not practice fall safety skills because they wish to consciously avoid the thought of a fall incident are more likely to freeze or not respond properly in an emergency.

ACKNOWLEDGEMENTS

I would like to gratefully acknowledge everyone who has contributed directly and indirectly to this book, many of whom have contributed substantial time and expertise.

There are many horse industry professionals I thank for their encouragement, support, and valuable feedback, all of which has ensured that the content and context of the book is relevant to riders across many disciplines: Gillian Rolton, dual Olympic eventing gold medallist; Joy Poole, President of the Australian Horse Industry Council; Diane Bennit, a Director of the Australian Horse Industry Council and horse safety consultant; Karlie Triffitt, Training Manager at the Australian Racing and Equine Academy; Wayne Boyde, Head Teacher at the Australian Racing and Equine Academy; Lisa Coffey, qualified instructor of equestrian and trackwork riders and Workforce Development Officer at Racing Victoria; Inez Musgrave, Executive Director of the Australian Jumps Racing Association; Michael Fenton, international racing expert/consultant and former stipendiary steward; Nina Arnott, Executive Officer at Horse Safety Australia; Jade Salpietro, founder of the Confident Rider website; Joe Curran, President of NSW Polo Association; Jeremy Bayard, polo player, for sharing his recent fall experience and acknowledging the benefit of fall safety training; Peter and Serena White, Scone Polo Club; Dianne Cullen, President of the Pony Club Association of NSW; Jamie Dowling, Director of the Southern Campdrafting Association; Josh Rodder, Racing Executive at Melbourne Racing Club; Helen Webster, President of Northside Riding Club; Deborah Lovett, teacher and equestrian coordinator at Hillcrest Christian College; Leanne Haywood, experienced rider and eventing coach; Kiwa Fisher, councillor and respected equestrian industry professional; and James Kay, teacher of equine studies and agriculture at TAFE NSW.

A number of highly experienced jockeys and former jockeys have been kind enough to discuss their significant experience in race falls with me. Thank you to Greg Childs—VIPA Safety, Peter Hutchinson—mentor for riders at Racing Victoria, Hugh Bowman, Jim Cassidy, Luke Nolan, Tommy Berry, Matt Neilson, James Winks, David Tootell, Jessica Valas, Jeff Penza, Matt Pumpa, and Kassie Furness.

'Hutchy'—1992 Cox Plate race fall—photo courtesy of Peter Hutchinson.

Thank you to a great team of doctors and specialist consultants who have substantial expertise and experience in their fields of endeavour: Dr Caron Jander, Consultant Occupational Physician and Former National Medical Officer for the Australian Racing Board; Dr Peta Hitchens, an expert on the epidemiology of jockey falls and equestrian injuries; Dr Rob Jackson, retired lecturer in English at the University of Sydney, for the many hours he spent proof-reading and improving the manuscript; Dr Tom Gibson, consultant biomechanist and director of Human Impact Engineering; Dr Stephen Pigott, Chairman of the British Medical Equestrian Association; Dr John Yeo, retired director of the Spinal Research Foundation; Dr Russell Roberts, consultant psychologist and director of Kumano Consulting; Grant Brecht, specialist sport psychologist and director of Elite Insight Performance Psychology; and Professor Lesley Day, former head of falls prevention research at Monash University Research Institute.

To my gymnastics and high-performance sport friends and colleagues, I thank them for their encouragement, suggestions for improvement or peer review of the skills and progressions: Ken Armanasco, a former gymnastic coach of state and national champions and director of Safety Dynamics—consultants in workplace safety; Andrew Cordery, High Performance Manager at Gymnastics SA; Alida Scott, former international gymnast and coach; Kym Dowdell, Chief Executive Officer at Gymnastics Queensland; Barry Cheales, Olympic gymnast and former national coach; Anne Marie Harrison, Chief Executive Officer at Victorian Institute of Sport; James Karageorgiou, Senior Physical Preparation Coach at Victorian Institute of Sport and former track-work rider; Frances Crampton, Sport Management Consultant and former international level gymnast and Olympic team coach; Jamie Parsons, Chief Executive Officer at Gymnastics Victoria; Aaron Bloomfield, Chief Executive Officer at Gymnastics NSW; Haydn Bellamy, State Director at Gymnastics SA; and Ruth Gibbons, Executive Director at Gymnastics WA.

I am also fortunate to have some great friends and supporters who have professional writing experience and/or have worked in journalism. They have given me the benefit of their skills and valuable feedback. Thank you to Tony Ryan, editor, Vanessa Hein, public relations consultant; Bill West, journalist; Susan Taylor, teacher and editor; Catrina McDonald; and Ron Lee, the Corporate Ninja, for his advice.

Thank you to Natasha Jackson for her excellent naturalistic drawing skills in depicting fall scenarios and movement sequences that could not otherwise be shown. Thank you to Richard Kennard, director of Horseland; and Joe McInally, renowned equestrian industry photographer, for assisting with the cover photo.

Thank you to my family for their support: my wife Jenny; our son Morgan; daughter Freya; and our son Riley for his demonstration of the many body shapes, exercises, skills and learning progressions to illustrate the techniques.

INTRODUCTION

It is not enough to know how to ride; you must know how to fall.

—from a Mexican proverb

History

Gymnastics and horse riding have long and interesting histories, and their evolution continues today with the development of new technologies and skills.

Gymnastics was first practiced in ancient Greece and included skills for mounting and dismounting a horse. Alexander the Great and his Macedonians are said to have practiced mounting and dismounting on a wooden horse, and Roman soldiers used wooden horses in their training.

The modern equestrian sport of eventing evolved from the use of warhorses for military training. The sport of equestrian vaulting dates back to ancient times and was referred to as 'artistic riding'. It was included as a sport in the 1920 Olympic Games in Antwerp. The sport of equestrian vaulting was developed in post-war Germany as a means of introducing children to equestrian sports (British Equestrian Vaulting, 2011).

Gymnastics exercises with wooden horses have also been practiced as part of military training to improve battle fitness. From the gymnastic horses used for this purpose, the modern-day pommel horse was developed.

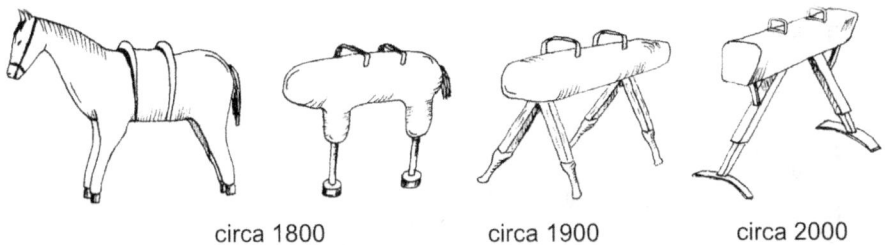

circa 1800   circa 1900   circa 2000

Research and Studies

Research has been conducted to help reduce injuries for riders, most of which are a result of a fall from a horse and many of which occur during training. (Cowley et al., 2007). Petridou et al. (2004) found that falls accounted for 67 per cent of horse-related injuries in farming, 88 per cent in sport, and 85 per cent in racing. Younger riders from about age fifteen to mid-twenties appear to carry the greatest risk of catastrophic horse-related injury (Cripps, 2000).

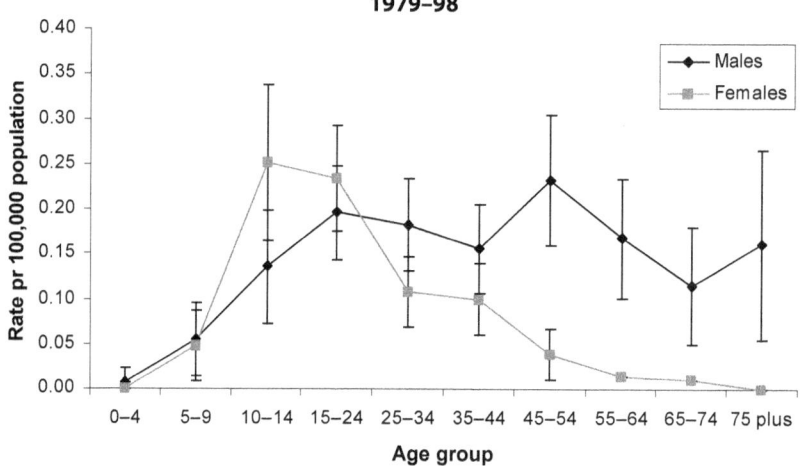

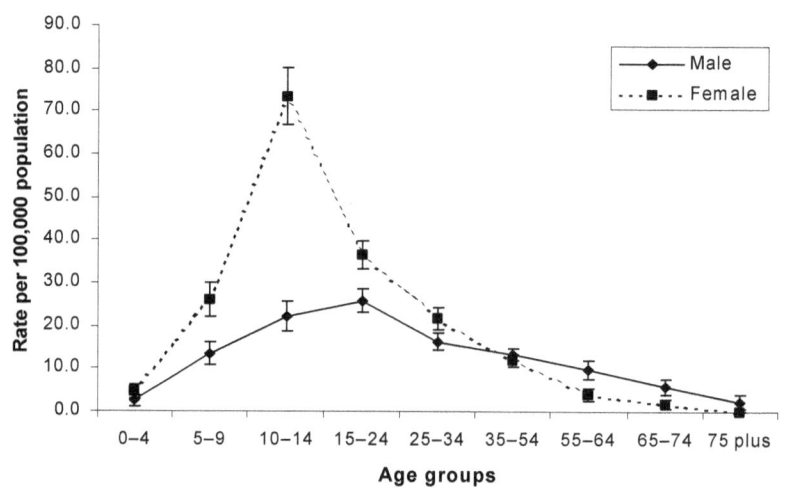

Source: *Australian Injury Prevention Bulletin No. 24, Horse-related injury in Australia*, Raymond Cripps, 2000.

In Australia alone, there has been an average of ten hospitalisations per day over a three-year period from 2008 to 2011—mostly due to horse riding activity, and from 2000 to 2012, there were ninety-eight horse-related deaths, of which 74 per cent—six per year—were a result of a fall from a horse (Safe Work Australia, 2014). Riders involved in jumping activities, such as hurdle and steeplechase racing, showjumping, cross-country, and point-to-pointing, are at the greatest risk of injury (Triantafyllopoulos et al., 2013).

Of all the equestrian activities, the competitive sports of eventing, showjumping, and cross-country are considered the riskiest. A horse that impacts a jumps obstacle and subsequently falls, either landing on or rolling over the rider, carries a high risk of a serious crush injury.

A report by Denzil O'Brien (2016), on the obstacles to risk calculation in the equestrian sport of eventing, collected information on fifty-nine rider deaths in eventing since 1993 across all levels of the sport. The fifty-nine fatalities (twenty-five males and thirty-four females) ranged in age from 12 to 64, with a median age of 32. The causes of these deaths are as follows: thirty-eight due to crush injury; eleven due to impact with the ground; nine where the injury mechanism was unknown or not reported; and one due to impact with a tree. Fatalities by country were England twenty-two, USA twelve, Australia five, France four, Germany three, Ireland three, Italy two, and one from Austria, Belgium, Portugal, Qatar, Russia, Scotland, Spain, and Sweden.

Horse racing is also considered one of the highest-risk sports (Hitchens et al., 2009). Hitchens et al. (2010) found factors that increase the risk of falls in racing include:

- being an apprentice jockey or amateur rider,
- lacking rider fitness,
- riding younger and less accomplished or less experienced horses,
- racing in shorter distance races, and
- riding on drier tracks where horse speed is greater and the surface is firmer.

Improvement in safety has most recently focused on areas such as helmets and body protectors, matching rider skill level with horse age and behaviour, modifying race railings to make them more collapsible, and changing rules and regulations to reduce the likelihood of falls (Northey, 2006). Breakable devices and deformable obstacles have also been used to improve safety where a horse impacts a jumps obstacle (FEI Eventing Risk Management Seminar, 2015).

However, there have occasionally been unwanted consequences of efforts to improve safety, including decreased rider competence in how to fall and increased percentage of serious injuries for riders wearing air jackets (FEI Eventing Risk Management Seminar, 2015 and 2016). Also of concern is an overly restrictive body protector that impedes a rider's ability to move into a tuck position (Foote et al., 2014).

An Australian study investigated video footage of seventeen falls by jockeys in various races. There were thirty-nine individual injuries from these falls, which included eight to the back or spine, seven to the head (two of which were fatal), six to the neck, six to the hip and lower limbs, five to the face, three to the chest, two to the shoulder or clavicle, and two to the upper limbs. There were observed to be very few proactive attempts at injury minimisation by riders, such as taking a tucked position. In a tucked position, the head and arms are 'tucked', or pulled closely to the body, and the spine flexed. The intent is to minimise flail of the limbs and reduce exposure of the neck when the jockey tumbles from the fall. The riders tended to hold onto the reins for as long as is possible and hence were poorly prepared for the eventual landing. When they tumbled, it was often uncontrolled, with arms and legs flailing (Foote et al., 2014).

Fall Safety Training

There has been no longitudinal study or research published on the training of riders in proper fall safety techniques and evidence-based evaluation of their potential for reducing injury rates. A study by Monash University Accident Research Centre on the prevention of equestrian injuries included the following conclusion on the use of falling techniques:

> *Little work seems to have been done on evaluating the effectiveness of teaching and using falling techniques. This countermeasure may offer a cheap and effective avenue of reducing a wide range of injuries, including those to the head, neck, and upper extremities (Finch et al., 1996).*

A Winston Churchill Fellowship report by Dr Caron Jander studied recent improvements in international health protection standards for jockeys in the UK, Ireland, France, and Germany and recommended enhancements to Australian practices. Among its recommendations were that apprentice jockeys be trained in how to fall. Apprentice jockeys in France are taught the basics of rolling and somersaulting, including the use of a mechanical-pneumatic horse, Equichute, to simulate a forward fall at speed (Jander, 2009).

In the UK, the British Racing School offers a training course to assist riders with falling technique (British Racing School, 2014). The Medical Equestrian Association in the UK suggests that fall training can make some behaviour second nature—crucial when there is only a split second to react (Medical Equestrian Association, 2012).

In 2013, following serious eventing falls and fatalities in Germany, working groups were created to look at a number of projects to improve safety, including fall training, and the construction of a mechanical horse used for teaching balance and improving of seat (FEI Eventing Risk Management Seminar, 2016).

Dispelling Some Myths

There is no time to respond in a fall

Fall times vary depending on the nature of the incident. Riders generally have an average of ¾ of a second (ranging from half a second to about one second) before they hit the ground. This is indeed a very short time. However, observations from other sports (such as baseball and gymnastics) show that people are able to respond in this timeframe providing they have been trained. Training in fall safety techniques will significantly improve a rider's ability to respond quickly in most falls and reduce the risk of serious injury. The training in initial emergency response action outlined in this book has been designed so that the rider only needs to make a single conscious decision to react on realisation that they are falling. The initial emergency response action can be carried out in half a second.

There is no time to respond in a high-speed fall

The time it takes to reach the ground when falling is a function of the height from which the rider falls. Vertical fall time is not diminished by the horizontal speed of travel. The additional forces at play in a high-speed fall, such as horizontal speed and angular momentum, are far greater than the forces in a low-speed fall. Training in fall safety techniques is even more important in high-speed falls due to the increased forces that riders are subjected to in these situations. In a high-speed fall, it is easy for fear, confusion, or conscious analysis to 'override' a rider's ability to respond without hesitation. Fall safety training will assist the rider to make a quick decision to respond, to reduce blunt force impact to the head and spine. Tuck-and-roll techniques will further mitigate the risk of injury in a fall when landing at speed.

Falling off my horse is failure; if I think about this or do the training, I might fall off my horse more often

Naturally, riders do not want to focus on the topic of falling off their horse, nor perhaps be reminded of the risks, or of any traumatic experiences they may have had. Fall safety training is an injury countermeasure, and top athletes and sportspeople do everything they can to reduce their risk of injury and the time-off that is required for rehabilitation. Many successful sportspeople in fields such as swimming, cycling, football, gymnastics, and athletics use strategies such as cross-training to aid recovery and prevent injury. Cross-training is a strategy where athletes do some training in another sport to assist in physical recovery, complementary skills development, and reducing the boredom from repetitive activities. These proactive injury prevention strategies lead to success, and do not passively ignore the reality that participation in sporting activity carries a risk of injury. What differentiates top-ranked sports people is often not how they deal with their successes, but how they learn and recover from their failures. Furthermore, fall safety skills are not horse riding skills, and no changes are required or suggested to any horse riding skills or practices. The initial emergency response action detailed in this book requires the rider to make a conscious decision to let go of the reins once a fall becomes *inevitable*. This will not result in riders falling off their horse more often. In addition to providing some protection in a fall, the training will have a positive impact on rider fitness levels and will also improve balance, general coordination, and kinaesthetic awareness—things that are likely to improve riders' fitness and ability to stay on their horse.

The skills need to be practiced every day to be of benefit

Once learned, fall safety skills do not need to be practiced daily to benefit riders. Some riders may have benefited from training in activities such as martial arts, gymnastics, or tumbling techniques, and some may have learned techniques such as letting go of the reins and performing a tuck-and-roll in a fall. Other riders may not have successfully mastered these techniques or transferred their skills from other activities to a horse riding fall. Training in proper fall safety techniques will improve riders' ability to transfer skills in other complementary activities to a fall. Once fall safety skills are learned and a rider has been able to apply their learning to a fall, the techniques will be retained for a significant period of time. As with most learning, there will be a loss of skill over time, but riders who are active can do some simple things to facilitate longer-term retention, including:

- a brief safety routine before each ride to reinforce skill retention and muscle memory, and
- participation in periodic follow-up training (each six to twelve months).

Many professionals are required to undertake safety training every year (as in first aid training), though most people would never have to apply these skills. Even if there is some loss of skill over time, being trained is better than being untrained.

It would benefit some horse riding activities, but not my activity

The speed, skills, and practices for different horse riding activities vary significantly, but the fall safety skills required to protect the rider in a fall do not. Once a rider becomes unseated and/or airborne, with a fall becoming inevitable, riding skills become irrelevant and what matters is how the rider responds once they realise they are going to fall. The initial emergency response, which includes letting go of the reins and moving the arms quickly into the brace position, is important for riders of all disciplines to protect their head and neck. Except perhaps for riders who are engaged in recreational activities—such as riding an older, predictable horse that is being led by a guide in a low-risk environment—every rider is exposed to a risk of falling from their horse. More likely to fall from their horse on a number of occasions are riders who regularly participate in higher-risk activities such as racing, rodeo, track-work, cross-country, showjumping, point-to-pointing, riding at speed, and other competitive sports such as polo. Fall safety training for riders who engage in these activities is very important as a countermeasure against serious injury.

Try to relax as much as possible in a fall

It is important not to resist or stop horizontal momentum in a fall when travelling at speed. This is very different from relaxing as much as possible. Riders must maintain the correct body shape and use muscle tension: first, to provide some protection for the head, neck, and spine from blunt force impact with the ground, and second, to dissipate the forces as a result of horizontal speed and angular

Introduction

momentum by using a tuck-and-roll technique. Correct body shape and muscle tension is the best way to provide some protection for the most important parts of the skeletal system—the skull and vertebrae—which in turn protect the brain and spinal cord.

I have done gymnastics/martial arts, so there is no need to do this training

Training in general gymnastics, martial arts, or tumbling skills is beneficial for riders for a number of reasons both physical and mental. General training of this nature is certainly better than being untrained in any such activity. The fall safety training outlined in this book is based on gymnastic skills and training methods, but has been adapted specifically to protect the rider in a fall. This includes training in areas such as:

- letting go of the reins and quickly moving the arms into the brace position when a fall becomes inevitable,
- simulation exercises to facilitate transfer of skills to a horse riding fall,
- repetition to develop spontaneous response action, and
- skill retention exercises such as a pre-ride safety routine.

Riders understand that horse riding skills vary considerably from one discipline to another. Learning the basics of how to ride a horse is important for all horse riding activities, but these basics are not sufficient to enable the rider to compete in a race at high-speed with many horses in close proximity. The skills required for equestrian dressage are very different from those required for showjumping, and a skilled jockey would need additional training and skills development for rodeo or to herd cattle in a campdraft or participate in a polo tournament. To gain the skills required for a higher level of protection in a fall, riders need to undertake specific training in fall safety, including simulation activities. Some of these activities can be specifically tailored to the rider's discipline, facilitating the transfer of skills.

Polo players observing a demonstration of the tuck-and-roll position

Top Dog

During a recent fall safety seminar at Windsor Polo Club in Australia, participants and a dog, 'Rover' (name changed to protect participant privacy☺), were observing a demonstration of the tuck-and-roll position.

Rover, after attentively observing the demonstration, came over to the tumbling mats and rolled onto his back with paws tucked-in. This was met by instant applause (and laughter) from all present.

> Homo sapiens can learn fall safety skills too!

Safety Considerations

All physical activities carry a risk of injury, including serious injury, such as when coming down from a height. The risk of injury to riders can be significantly mitigated by:

- evidence-based research,
- analysis of fall scenarios,
- mental and physical preparation,
- recovery techniques,
- safety equipment, and
- continuous improvement strategies.

Training in fall safety for riders, despite the negative feeling it may trigger for some who have fallen from their horse, is low-risk compared to actual horse riding. Any negative feelings about the training should quickly dissipate once riders commence and realise that learning the skills can be fun, and can provide some protection against serious injury in a fall. The training methods detailed in this book do not involve falling from real horses. Many of the skills and training methods have been modified from those of standard gymnastics techniques to maximise safety in a fall, and should be included as an essential part of an overall safety strategy for riders.

Well-designed fall safety training can simulate some real fall scenarios closely, without the need to increase the risk of injury by introducing real horse work. Some of the more advanced simulations can be achieved by using equipment such as a modified bicycle or a replica or mechanical horse, and by performing skills close to the horse riding environment.

Before starting any training program, riders should be confident that they do not have any health or medical limitations that might increase the risk of injury during training. This is no different from general fitness or sports training, where the same principles apply. If riders have any concerns, such as a previous neck or back injury, consult a medical practitioner and then discuss with a fall safety instructor any limitations or modifications to training that may be needed.

Fall safety instructor ('qualified instructor')

A number of skills and activities can be learned and practiced by riders simply by following the training methods in this book. Other skills and activities require the supervision of an instructor who is qualified to teach the skills. Fall safety skills and activities are not riding skills or practices, and they will only come into play when a rider is falling from their horse. Instructors who have the experience and qualifications to teach fall safety skills are likely to come from sports such as gymnastics, tumbling, or martial arts. In this book, a 'qualified instructor' is one who is qualified to teach fall safety skills and activities. It does not mean 'horse riding instructor'.

If everything is fine from a medical perspective, riders should also review their current fitness and skill level, and any prior experience in a similar type of training with their qualified instructor. This will enable a better understanding of their starting fitness level and their plan for the progressive learning of fall safety skills.

The training involves warm-up, basic skills, body-shaping activities, some physical conditioning exercises and—for those riders who are ready to progress—some more advanced skills and simulations. Riders who improve their fitness and physical conditioning will be in a better position to actively respond in a fall. Physical conditioning complements skill learning.

Working with a qualified instructor is the best way to safely learn the more advanced skills and simulations. There are, however, a number of basic activities and exercises that riders can learn and practice without supervision following the methods in this book. Learning these basics will afford more protection than being untrained.

Each skill described in this book includes details of prerequisites (if any), an illustration of the movement sequence, and a list of key technical points. Progression should always be managed carefully and supervised by a qualified instructor. As a general rule, before progressing, a skill should be performed consistently well for a number of repetitions and, for more advanced skills, over multiple training sessions. Both the rider and the qualified instructor should be confident in progressing to the next level. Some skills may require spotting (where the qualified instructor provides some physical assistance with the activity as required), or the use of equipment such as a safety belt and/or a crashmat during the early stages of learning.

Most riders will gain some benefit from a single training session, and ten training sessions of two hours duration should enable most riders to significantly improve their skill level. After ten training sessions, riders should discuss their progress with their fall safety instructor to decide whether additional training should be carried out. Some follow-up training to facilitate skills retention should be carried out at least annually, but preferably on a six-monthly basis.

Remember:

- Some training is better than no training at all.
- Read and understand the theory and science—knowledge is power.
- Include some warm-up and conditioning exercises in your normal routine. The fitter you are, the less severe your injuries may be if you fall.
- Some basic drills and skills can be done safely without supervision. The more you practice these basics, the better prepared you will be in a fall.
- Repetition of basics improves muscle memory and retention of skills.
- If you are returning from a break or from an injury, go back to the basics, consult your medical practitioner and qualified instructor, and then repeat the basic skills and conditioning exercises.

Rider Self-help Guide: How to Use This Book

Riders will benefit from increased knowledge and understanding by reading the Introduction and Theory and Science sections of this book. Armed with greater knowledge of fall safety techniques, riders will be in a better position to dispense with some commonly held myths and false beliefs that may exist in relation to falling from a horse. Improved understanding is an important precursor to riders avoiding the influence of unqualified (though often well-intentioned) opinions that may make matters worse in a fall.

Some riders may have developed skills in activities such as martial arts, tumbling, gymnastics, or other complementary activities. Some basic simulations, such as letting go of the reins, will assist riders to apply already developed skills to a fall scenario.

Basics include warm-up activities, the brace position, basic rolling skills, letting go of the reins, feet-first landing practice, jumping and landing from various heights, and conditioning exercises (such as neck, arm, and middle-body conditioning). There are over ten basic activities/skills that can be easily practiced following the methods in this book, without the need for specialised equipment or supervision. Practicing these basics will afford riders more protection than being untrained.

Activities that can be practiced without the supervision of a qualified instructor are labelled as follows in the sections 'Skill Learning and Training Methods' and also 'Vaulting Skills and Simulation Activities':

> Safe to do unsupervised

Despite being generally safe to learn these basics unsupervised, please note the 'Safety Considerations' in the previous section before beginning any training program.

Once mastered with the assistance of a qualified instructor, additional rolling and tumbling skills, some additional simulation activities, and the pre-ride safety routines can also be practiced without supervision. Consult a qualified instructor to determine readiness to practice additional skills unsupervised. These skills and activities are labelled as follows:

> Safe to do unsupervised
> once mastered

After an injury, a significant break from training, a change in health or fitness level, or a loss of confidence to perform the skills, you should consult a medical practitioner and/or qualified instructor before practicing the skills. All other skills and activities should be learned and practiced under the supervision of a qualified instructor.

Rider self-help activities and skills are detailed in the following sections of the book:

Safe to do unsupervised

Topic	Page
Warm-up and conditioning exercises	53
Body shapes and positions	62
Basic rolling and tumbling skills	
• Forward roll	70
• Sideways shoulder roll	72
• Egg roll	73
Basic aerial skills	
• Basic jumps	79
Fall simulation activities	
• Letting go of the reins and brace position	125

Equipment: the recommended equipment for learning the above skills includes: an exercise mat—dimensions 2.4 × 1.2 m × 40 mm (8 × 4 ft × 1.6 in)—and reins + tent peg. For the skills listed below, a vinyl covered foam block—dimensions 120 × 90 × 60 cm (4 × 3 × 2 ft)—is also recommended.

Safe to do unsupervised once mastered

Topic	Page
Rolling and tumbling skills	
• Backward roll	74
• Handstand roll	76
Aerial skills	
• Jump, land, and roll	83
Dive roll drills and skills	
• Dive roll drill	75
• Standing dive roll	100
• Dive roll from an approach run	102
Replica horse simulations	
• Emergency dismount practice	127
Pre-ride safety routines	141

All other skills and activities should be learned and practiced under the supervision of a qualified instructor.

Fall Safety Instructor Guide: How to Use This Book

The skills and activities for rider fall safety training are based on gymnastics techniques. There are, however, a number of important differences from traditional gymnastics that maximise safety in a fall. It is important that these modifications and their purpose are understood by qualified instructors who teach riders the fall safety skills detailed in this book.

Riders may have taught themselves some fall safety skills. Periodic testing—of skills, fitness, and anthropometric measures—is recommended to check riders' progress and motivate them to train further and improve their skills. When progressing to more advanced techniques, continue to practice the basics, including warm-up and other activities. Riders will have different aptitude levels for learning fall safety skills, so it is important that group training sessions allow individuals to progress at their own rates.

The sections 'Skill Learning and Training Methods' followed by 'Vaulting Skills and Simulation Activities' detail the techniques and guidelines for progression. Many of the more advanced skills are simply a progression or variation on previously developed skills, expanding on the rider's repertoire and enabling them to respond more intuitively in a fall.

Height Progression—Guidelines

	Level	Examples
Low	Ground level	Forward roll
Moderate	60 cm (2 ft)	Dive roll from jog
High	120 cm (4 ft)	Dive roll from height
Advanced	150 to 180 cm (5 to 6 ft)	Dive roll over obstacle

Speed Progression—Guidelines

	Approach Method	Speed	Horse Gait
Stationary	From standing	0	Standing
Low	Jog	to 10 km/h (6 mph)	Walk/jog
Moderate	Run	to 20 km/h (12 mph)	Trot/canter
High	Fast run/sprint	to 30 km/h (18 mph)	Slow gallop

Landing Surface Progression—Guidelines

	Surface	Mat Thickness
Crashmat*	Soft (low density)	30 cm (12 in)
Landing Mat	Moderate (medium density)	15 cm (6 in)
Tumbling Mat	Firm (high density)	5 cm (2 in)
Grass/turf**	Hard (some give in ground surface)	0

* A crashmat provides some additional protection against injury when learning. It cannot protect the rider from all landing injuries and is not a substitute for qualified instruction and proper skills progression.

** Before practicing on a grass/turf surface, the ground should be inspected to ensure that there are no hazards such as holes, rock, glass, uneven surfaces, underlying concrete, or protrusions such as metal or tree roots. The grass/turf surface should have some give. Riders should wear their regulation protective clothing, e.g. helmet and body protector, when practicing on hard landing surfaces.

In some horse riding activities, riders may be riding on very hard surfaces such as a road, on bitumen, or on hard ground. It is not necessary or recommended to practice on these very hard surfaces, as it will increase the risk of injury in training. The skills required to land on very hard surfaces are the same as those for landing on grass/turf or softer surfaces.

Progression for many of the skills involves gradually increasing the height and/or speed and transitioning from soft to harder landing surfaces. Skills should be performed well before progression in height, speed or landing surface.

The above progression parameters are guidelines only. Do not feel compelled to keep progressing beyond the rider's fitness, skill, or confidence levels. Riders who have a lower fitness level should progress at a slower rate. The height progression should also be paced according to age, fitness level and riding activity. There is no need, for example, for young pony riders to jump from a height of 150 cm (5 ft), where they are not riding at this height.

Even if a rider only develops their skill at low height, low speed, and on softer landing surfaces, they will be in a better position to respond in a fall to mitigate the risk of injury than they would be if not trained.

THEORY AND SCIENCE

Spontaneity isn't random. . . . How good people's decisions are under the fast moving, high stress condition of rapid cognition is a function of training and rules and rehearsal.

—Malcolm Gladwell (2005)
Blink: The Power of Thinking without Thinking

Fall and Response Times

Fall Times

Fall times to the ground are predictable and are based on the height that the rider is falling from. Vertical fall time in a free fall is not diminished by the horizontal speed of travel. The time it takes to impact the ground when falling is independent of horizontal speed and is a function of gravity, the height of the fall, and whether the rider impacts their horse or some other obstacle before hitting the ground.

Fall time in this book is expressed in milliseconds (ms), where 1 second = 1,000 ms, and

¾ of a second = 750 ms
½ of a second = 500 ms
¼ of a second = 250 ms

CALCULATION OF FALL TIME

Fall Time (ms) = [Square Root of (2 × H / G)] × 1000

Where: H = height of fall in metres; and
G = fall acceleration due to gravity = 9.8 (m/s^2)

Height	Formula (metric)	Fall time
3.0 m (9.8 ft)	Sqrt (2 × 3.0 / 9.8) × 1000	782 ms
2.5 m (8.2 ft)	Sqrt (2 × 2.5 / 9.8) × 1000	714 ms
2.0 m (6.6 ft)	Sqrt (2 × 2.0 / 9.8) × 1000	639 ms
1.5 m (4.9 ft)	Sqrt (2 × 1.5 / 9.8) × 1000	553 ms
1.25 m (4.1 ft)	Sqrt (2 × 1.25 / 9.8) × 1000	505 ms

With the average horse height being about 160 cm (5.2 ft), or 16 hands, and a rider's centre of gravity being about 40 cm (16 in) above this height, the average height of rider falls is approximately 2.0 m (6.6 ft). The fall time to the ground in a free fall from 2.0 metres (6.6 ft) is 639 ms. Fall times vary depending on the height of the horse, the rider's position at the commencement of the fall, and the body shape of the rider when they impact the ground. For example, in a 4-point landing body shape, fall time and vertical impact force will be slightly less than when landing in a prone position from the same height.

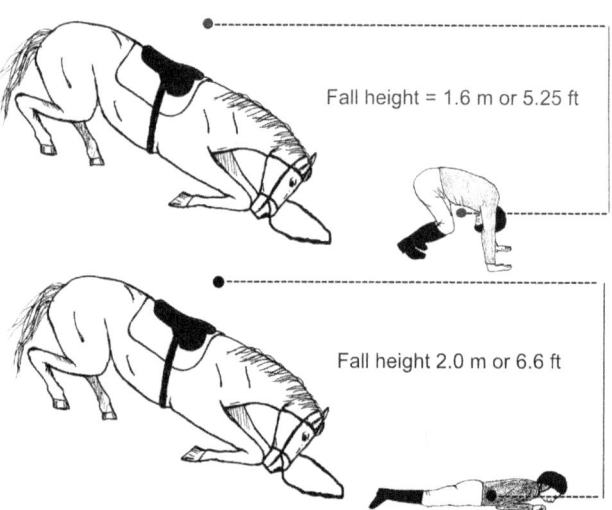

Sometimes a rider may be bucked into the air, in which case the height of the fall will increase. In other situations, where a horse has downward momentum at the time the rider becomes dislodged, the rider may be falling from a lower height with less fall time. The actual fall time to the ground can be accurately determined by frame-by-frame video analysis of falls where video evidence is available.

Now let's examine the likely effect of the horse variable on fall times. The following fall times have been calculated from the time the rider first commences falling to the point where the rider makes initial contact with the ground. Video analysis of a sample of falls reveals the following:

Jockey Fall Times in Race Falls (Nylund, 2016)

Case	**Fall Time**	
Jockey 1	1,040 ms	(1 second)
Jockey 2	967 ms	
Jockey 3	880 ms	
Jockey 4	760 ms	
Jockey 5	760 ms	
Jockey 6	709 ms	
Jockey 7	701 ms	
Jockey 8	680 ms	
Jockey 9	665ms	
Jockey 10	500 ms	(half second)
Average:	**766 ms**	

Rider Fall Times in Showjumping and Cross-country Events (Nylund, 2016)

Case	Fall Time	
Rider 1	1,334 ms	(1.3 seconds)
Rider 2	1,100 ms	
Rider 3	1,097 ms	
Rider 4	900 ms	
Rider 5	800 ms	
Rider 6	800 ms	
Rider 7	734 ms	
Rider 8	667 ms	
Rider 9	600 ms	
Rider 10	553 ms	(half second)
Average:	**856 ms**	

Evident from the above is that the variation in fall times when falling from or with a horse in showjumping or cross-country falls, first, increases the range and variance of fall times and, second, increases the average fall time to the ground when compared to the free fall times from heights of 1.25 to 3.0 m (4 to 10 ft). An analysis of the above videos reveals that a rider's downward momentum is sometimes temporarily interrupted as a result of the rider impacting the horse as they fall, and this is one reason for the increased fall times in some scenarios. The other factor that can increase fall times in jumps is where the rider falls from a greater height. However, in most of these cases, the rider impacted their horse in some way as they fell, so this was the more significant factor in the increased fall times for riders involved in jumps activities.

The effect of jockeys impacting their horse as they fell appeared to increase the fall time by an average of approximately 130 ms in race falls when compared to the free fall time from a height of 2 m (6.6 ft)—639 versus 766 ms. The additional height and/or the effect of riders impacting their horse as they fell in equestrian jumps activities, increased the average fall time by more than 200 ms when compared to the free fall time from a height of 2 m (6.6 ft)—639 versus 856 ms. It should be noted, however, that in some fall scenarios, for both racing and equestrian jumps, the rider did not impact their horse and fall times were essentially the free fall time. At faster horse speeds, where there is often a more abrupt change in velocity, it appears less likely that the rider will impact their horse as they fall.

Allowing for these variations, it is estimated that rider fall time in race falls is on average ¾ of a second and generally within the range of 500 to 1,000 ms (half a second to one second). In jumps, there is sometimes slightly more time available to the rider and fall times are estimated to generally be within a range of 500 to 1,300 ms (half a second to just over a second). These are indeed very short time frames, but they are long enough for riders who have been trained in fall safety skills to take emergency action to protect their head and neck in most fall scenarios. In other sports such as baseball, there is significantly less time to react. Baseball players need to make a decision within 250 milliseconds whether or not to strike a ball travelling at 95 mph (Exploratorium, 2016).

Response Time

Response time is the time a rider takes to react (reaction time) and then take action (movement time) to mitigate injury in a fall.

Response Time = Reaction Time + Movement Time

If we had the luxury of a lot of time in a fall, it might be possible to evaluate the scenario and choose between various courses of action. In half a second to one second, the rider does not have that benefit. The time available to the rider is nevertheless sufficient for response action. Once the rider recognises they are falling, it requires a snap decision without hesitation.

Malcolm Gladwell, in his book *Blink*, examines experiences from a number of fields of endeavour and explains the steps taken to shape, manage, and educate one's own unconscious reactions:

> *Snap judgements are, first of all, enormously quick: they rely on the thinnest slices of experience. But they are also unconscious ... snap judgments can be made in a snap because they are frugal, and if we want to protect our snap judgements, we have to take steps to protect that frugality.* (Gladwell, 2005)

The initial emergency response to let go of the reins and snap the arms into the brace position to protect the head and neck is a single emergency response action for all fall scenarios. This frugal action enables the rider to respond very quickly and, with practice, can be executed within half a second once the rider recognises that they are falling.

SIMPLE REACTION TIME

Simple reaction time is the time it takes to recognise a stimulus (when expecting the need to react) and for our brain to send a signal to the muscles to respond. It does not include the actual movement time. Some examples of stimuli include:

- a starter's gun going off in an athletic race (auditory stimulus),
- a green light (visual stimulus),
- barrier gates opening in a horse race (visual and auditory stimulus), and
- a foot coming out of a stirrup (kinaesthetic stimulus).

Research on reaction times indicates that simple adult reaction times generally fall within a range of 130 to 220 ms.

Study	Subjects	Time (ms)
Pilianidis, T. et al. (2012)	Olympic sprinters/hurdlers	146–210
Gavkare, A. et al. (2013)	Undergraduate students & athletes	134–144
Kosinski, R. (2008)	University students	160–190
Deng, S. et al. (2006)	High school students	160–220
Hitchens, P. et al. (2011)	Jockeys and track-work riders	192–215

Taking into account individual differences, 250 ms (a quarter of a second) is an allowance for simple adult reaction time (for age 16 to 60), which should account for the vast majority of adult horse riders, particularly those involved in higher-risk activities.

Reaction times are slower in children. Hope et al. (2015) reported mean simple reaction times of 380 ms for 7—9 year olds, 317 ms for 10—12 year olds, and 304 ms for 13—15 year olds. Simple reaction times peak (are fastest) from age 20 to 30. From age 30 onwards, reaction time remains relatively stable with a slight decline from age 50 to 60 and a more marked decline after age 60 (Der et al., 2006). Females are generally reported to have slower reaction times than males. However, the differences in simple reaction times based on gender appear to be minor and have been included in the above simple reaction times.

EXPECTANCY (Warning Signals)

Where there is some prior warning of a need to react, such as the starting official announcing 'set' in an athletics race, or watching a computer screen and being poised ready to click a mouse on seeing a green light, individuals can react very quickly. This is simple reaction time.

Sometimes, just prior to a fall, riders have some warning that there is a risk of falling. Some examples of warning signals include:

- the rider becomes unbalanced,
- the rider's foot comes out of a stirrup,
- a horse nearby or directly in front falls or stumbles,
- the horse is behaving erratically or not responding properly,
- the horse is jumping over an obstacle and has taken off poorly, or
- the rider sees a horse in front of them shift without allowing enough room.

In situations where there is some prior warning of a possible fall, a rider can react quickly once alerted to a problem. Where there is no prior warning, there is a delay (latency) in ability to react because the rider needs to change their focus of attention from 'riding' to 'falling'. Research on the effect of warning signals on subjects' reaction times confirms that reaction times following a warning signal are quicker than when there is no prior warning. Bertelson (1967) found that when there was a warning of 100 to 200 ms, reaction time was quicker than when there was no warning.

If we do not have the benefit of expectancy—with our focus of attention being on something else—then overall response time in a fall will be slower. In this situation, an additional allowance of time needs to be made for recognition of a fall. Riders are generally alert when riding, and taking into account Bertelson's research and the mental processing time in simple reaction time studies, an additional 200 ms will allow for latency in a rider's response in an unexpected fall.

EFFECT OF TRAINING ON RESPONSE TIME

Training has a significant positive effect on response time. Rogers et al. (2003) found that training older people to resist falls by stepping out to stabilise themselves improved their reaction times. In particular, training in fall safety skills can reduce overall response time in an emergency for a number of reasons. These include:

- improved fitness and muscle memory,
- improved recognition of what to do in an emergency,
- improved ability to quickly switch focus of attention if required,
- unconscious learning and improved ability to respond intuitively, and
- the creation of neural pathways that transfer skills from a simulation activity to a real fall scenario.

MOVEMENT TIME

Movement time is the time taken from the start of muscle contraction to the completion of a movement sequence. The time taken to complete a movement sequence will vary considerably depending on what movement is being performed. Frame-by-frame video analysis of movement sequences enables accurate measurement of movement times. Movement times for the same movement sequence will vary between individuals and can improve significantly with training. The movement time to get the arms into the brace position, with training, is approximately 250 ms.

ESTIMATED TOTAL RESPONSE TIME

Unexpected fall incident = 200 + 250 + 250 = 700 ms

This includes an allowance of 200 ms for latency of response in an unexpected fall, plus 250 ms for simple reaction time, plus 250 ms to let go of the reins and quickly move the arms into the brace position.

Incidents with warning of possible fall = 250 + 250 = 500 ms

Where there is warning of a possible fall, the reaction time may be reduced to simple reaction time in some scenarios. Response time in these scenarios is estimated to be 250 ms for simple reaction time plus 250 ms to let go of the reins and quickly move the arms into the brace position.

The above are estimated response times and some riders will be able to respond more quickly than this. Furthermore, the difference between a situation in which there is a warning and one in which there is no warning is not binary: there is a range of possibilities, from situations where there is little or no warning, to situations that provide some warning, to situations where there is a lot of warning. This means that response times will fall within a range of possible values depending on the individual and the scenario.

A horse may stumble before falling and attempt to regain its footing. Falls of this nature provide some warning of a likely fall and allow the rider to be poised to respond if necessary. Riders will also want to stay on their horse, regain their balance if possible, try to assist their horse to recover or wait to see if they or their horse can recover.

In some cases, these pre-fall warning signals do not last for long, sometimes only a few milliseconds. In other cases, pre-fall warning signals may last for a second or more. Video review of falls suggests that riders often have some warning signal of a possible fall, though the signal may only be brief.

CHOICE REACTION TIME

Having to choose between alternatives will add considerably to reaction time, compared with simple reaction time where only one conscious decision is being made, namely, to respond or not to respond. The additional time taken to react when there is more than one choice involved, results from the time it takes for the brain to process the information and choose between two or more options. Factors that delay ability to react in these situations include the number and nature of the situational variables and the number of possible choices that are being considered.

Balakrishnan et al. (2014) conducted a visual reaction time test involving choice, for 60 subjects of average age 19 years, where subjects had to hit one of three colour-coded buttons—red, green, or yellow. The average choice reaction time was between 500 and 550 ms. Based on what we know of simple visual reaction time, choice reaction time measured in this study slowed the response time by at least 250 ms (a quarter of a second) when compared with simple reaction time.

In a horse riding fall, there are many more situational variables and a greater level of complexity than the simple recognition of colours on a screen. Sternberg (1969) found that increasing the number of items in a simple recognition task added approximately 40 ms per additional item to mean reaction time. In a contextual-recall task, where the additional variable of position in a list of items was introduced, 114 ms was added to mean reaction time per item. This suggests that attempting to evaluate the circumstances of a fall—for example, 'is my horse falling, or am I falling but not my horse as well?'; 'should I hang onto or should I let go of the reins?' etc.—would require significantly more time than a rider has available in the majority of falls and particularly in an unexpected fall.

Too much conscious evaluation, when time is of the essence, can lead to 'paralysis through analysis' and an inability to carry out any protective response. The additional time required to evaluate and choose between different courses of action is significant when a rider only has half a second to one second available. For this reason, the recommended fall safety initial response action is a single initial emergency response action for all fall scenarios. This will enable the rider to respond very quickly to mitigate the risks of serious injury once they recognise they are falling, particularly if falling head or face first to the ground. The emergency response action does not require riders to choose between different alternatives or evaluate what is happening around them.

BENEFIT OF FALL SAFETY TRAINING BASED ON FALL TIMES

In most situations, with proper training in fall safety techniques, riders should be able to respond to protect themselves in a way that is better than taking no action at all. Fall safety training should be undertaken even if injury outcomes can be improved in some but not all falls.

The following graph gives an overview of the likely benefit of being trained in fall safety skills. Rider response time after training is estimated to be on average 500 ms where there is a warning signal that the rider may fall and 700 ms where the rider has no warning signal prior to the time they need to take action. Allowing for individual and situational differences, this benefit is expanded to a range of values plus or minus 100 ms (400 to 800 ms).

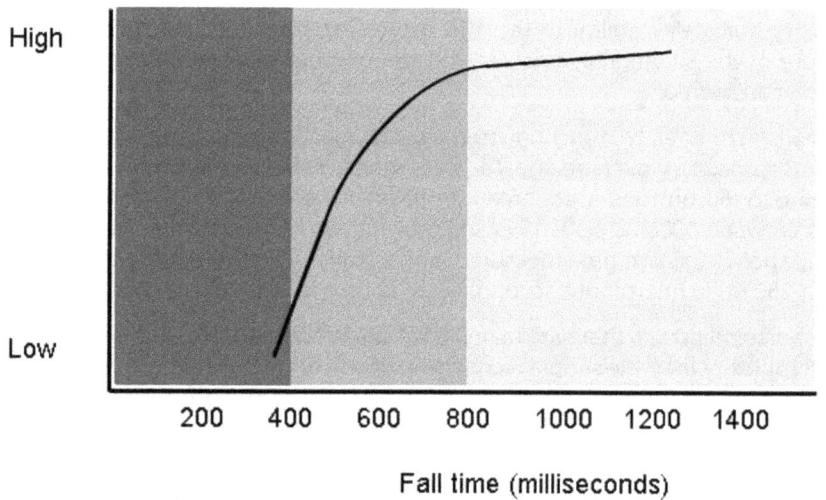

Because rider fall times are, greater than 500 ms in the vast majority of falls, it is evident that training in fall safety skills will enable riders to reduce their risk of serious injury.

Amanda Ripley, in her book *The Unthinkable: Who Survives When Disaster Strikes—and Why*, writes about the importance of training for disaster response:

> *Without too much trouble, we can teach our brains to work more quickly, maybe even more wisely, under great stress. We have more control over our fates than we think. But we need to stop underestimating ourselves.* (Ripley, 2009)

Spontaneity and Unconscious Learning

Spontaneity or 'unconscious learning', means that once subjected to a particular stimulus, or set of circumstances, a person can execute a response without the need for much conscious decision-making. The response can take place very quickly because it happens without the need for evaluation of circumstances other than recognition of falling. An experienced jockey—who has learned how to 'read the race'—making a snap decision to take advantage of an opening is an example of a spontaneous response action.

The stimulus may be physical, kinaesthetic (becoming unbalanced and falling), visual or auditory, or a combination of different stimuli. It can also be a mental trigger, an imagined stimulus—our unconscious thought process does not generally distinguish between what is real and what is imagined. If you have ever woken from a dream (possibly a nightmare) in a sweat or with your heart beating strongly, you will understand this blurring of the line between the imagined and the real: the imagined situation in a dream can trigger the same unconscious physiological reaction as a real situation. This demonstrates the power of our unconscious mind to influence our behaviour. By harnessing the power of the unconscious mind—when time is of the essence—riders can substantially improve their odds of protecting themselves in a fall and 'walking away'.

We know that simple adult human reaction time is on average about 200 ms. If, every time we had to perform a movement sequence, we needed to make a conscious decision to carry out every muscle action, it would be impossible for a gymnast to perform a somersault, for a batter to strike a baseball travelling at speed, for a rider to jump an obstacle or for a jockey to quickly take advantage of an opening in a race. In these examples, there are likely to be numerous muscle actions that need to be carried out in less than a second.

The reason we can perform complex skills quickly and easily is they become a learned response. A single conscious decision to react can trigger a learned movement sequence, just as clicking on a mouse button triggers the execution of software code (often including many sub-routines) almost instantaneously.

Our unconscious brain is like a powerful computer in which complex movement sequences can be performed very quickly—instead of computer code our brain works with neural networks.

The amount of training required to perform a skill without conscious thought varies from one individual to the next. Factors that affect how quickly an individual learns a movement sequence to execute it unconsciously include:

- coordination,
- physical capability,
- motivation to learn the skill,
- quality of training (technical merit),
- quantity of training (number of repetitions),
- starting skill level (prior training and experience),
- number of training sessions (spaced repetition), and
- physical preparation (strength/flexibility/endurance/muscle memory).

After 50 to 100+ repetitions, a movement sequence will start to become a less conscious process. For some basic skills, this can begin to happen over a few training sessions. It is important to note, however, that 50 repetitions of a skill in one training session will not result in the same learning outcome as 50 repetitions performed over multiple training sessions. Spaced repetition, with recovery intervals, will generally result in better long-term retention than a large amount of training at one time.

It is recommended that riders complete at least ten training sessions of approximately two hours each, with recovery intervals based on their fitness level, to learn fall safety skills so they become more intuitive. Some riders may need to do more training than this, and a qualified instructor can offer guidance.

As some of the fall safety skills are basic, everyone who is capable of riding a horse can develop their skills to a level that will afford more protection than being untrained. Basic skills include letting go of the reins and moving the arms quickly into the brace position, landing skills, basic rolling techniques, and physical conditioning exercises. Riders who perform the most basic recommended pre-ride safety routine, which can be learned after a few training sessions, will practice the brace position and some landing and rolling techniques prior to each ride. And it requires only a few minutes of their time! It will not be long before riders have repeated some of the basics more than 100 times, and this should enable them to respond more intuitively in a fall.

After ten training sessions, most riders should be able to perform the basics spontaneously, and many riders will also learn some of the more advanced skills in this time. Periodic follow-up training is recommended for skills retention.

It is worth noting that experience can have a significant effect on how well a skill is retained. Once the fall safety skills have been mastered, riders who have applied their skills in a fall are likely to retain them over a long period.

Spaced repetition is important to achieve unconscious learning where the skill has not been applied in a fall or where technique is important and refinement needs to take place.

Emergency Dismount

An emergency dismount is not the same as a fall, but it is an important skill. Riders who are competent in an emergency dismount may be able to avoid a more dangerous situation by taking proactive action. In an emergency dismount, the rider is making a conscious decision to dismount to avoid a more dangerous situation of remaining on a horse that is out of control and heading for danger, and which will possibly fall itself or throw the rider off.

Two emergency dismount scenarios are outlined: first, a lower-risk emergency dismount where the rider may decide to hang onto the reins to restrain the horse after dismounting, and second, a higher-risk emergency dismount where the safest option is to let go of the reins.

Different riding activities or disciplines carry different risks in situations where the rider may need to do an emergency dismount. Riders should consult with their riding instructor to understand the circumstances where an emergency dismount may be the safest option. Some general guidelines are outlined below.

Lower-risk Emergency Dismount

- the horse is travelling at low speed (a walk or slow trot),
- the rider has safe ground for landing,
- the rider is able to land feet-first,
- the rider has lost and unable to regain control of their horse, and
- there is a significant risk of increased danger by remaining on the horse.

It is recommended that riders practice a low-risk emergency dismount with assistance from their riding instructor (adhering to any additional advice) and on an older or more predictable horse. The rider should learn to do an emergency dismount from both sides of the horse.

An emergency dismount can be learned from a replica horse or from a stationary horse with the riding instructor restraining the horse. Once competent in an emergency dismount from both sides of a stationary horse, riders can progress their skill level by doing an emergency dismount at low speed (a walk). Before practicing an emergency dismount from a horse that is travelling at low speed, riders should, as a prerequisite, be competent in the following:

- feet-first landing,
- jumps from a height, land and roll forward,
- jumps from a height, land and roll sideways,
- emergency dismounts from both sides of a stationary horse.

The skill learning and progression to jump from a height, land and roll is detailed in the section 'Basic Aerial Skills'. Practice an emergency dismount while hanging onto the reins to restrain the horse (if safe to do so) and also practice an emergency dismount while letting go of the reins—as a preparation for a higher-risk emergency dismount scenario. As a safety precaution, riders should have the assistance of a riding instructor to ensure that the horse is restrained after the rider has dismounted.

It is not recommended that young or less-experienced riders hang onto the reins when doing an emergency dismount, even if the horse is stationary or travelling at low speed. Young or less-experienced riders may, first, not have gained the necessary experience to evaluate the circumstances of whether the situation is low or high-risk and, second, not be able to restrain the horse after landing, and so may end up dragged under or kicked by the horse.

Technique:

1. Quickly remove your feet from the stirrups.
2. Place your hands on the pommel or withers or neck and swing one leg backward and over the croup (hindquarters) of the horse and push away so you land clear.
3. Bend your knees when landing with the arms in the brace position.

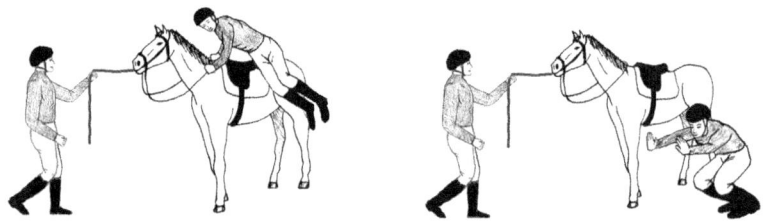

Emergency dismount practice with instructor assistance to restrain the horse

Once the rider is competent in a quick emergency dismount from both sides of a stationary horse, it will be beneficial to also practice the technique at low speed (a walk). Practice an emergency dismount with the assistance of a riding instructor to restrain the horse. Young and less-experienced riders should not hang onto the reins when practicing an emergency dismount.

Higher-risk Emergency Dismount

- the horse rears significantly,
- the rider has safe ground for landing,
- the horse is travelling at speed (such as a canter or gallop),
- the rider has lost and unable to regain control of their horse, and
- there is likely to be increased danger by remaining on the horse.

Technique (always let go of the reins in a higher-risk emergency dismount):

1. Quickly remove your feet from the stirrups, then let go of the reins.
2. Place your hands on the pommel or withers or neck and swing one leg backward over the croup (hindquarters) of the horse and push away so you land clear with the arms in the brace position.
3. If landing feet-first (the most likely scenario), bend your knees when landing and quickly move away from the horse, or
4. If landing at an angle or at speed, the arms should be in the brace position. If the rider is in a 'spread eagle' type position when coming off, they should quickly bring their legs together for landing and be ready to tuck-and-roll if necessary. A tuck position will mitigate the risk of injury if the rider falls and is forced to roll when landing at speed. The technique of land, tuck-and-roll should only be practiced in a low-risk environment with equipment such as a replica horse or with a riding instructor restraining the horse. The technique for doing an emergency dismount in a higher-risk situation is the same as the skill that can be learned and practiced in a lower-risk environment—there is no need to increase the risk of injury in order to learn the skill.

IMPORTANT SAFETY NOTE:

Dismounting a horse that is travelling at higher speed carries increased risk of injury. The above information is a general guideline only and riders should consult their riding instructor to understand the situations where an emergency dismount is a safer option than remaining on the horse. This will depend on the skills and experience of the rider, their horse and the environment they are riding in. It is important that riders have developed the skill of doing an emergency dismount in a safe environment before being in a situation where they may need to apply it in an emergency.

Fall Scenarios and Fall Safety Skills

Fall Scenarios

There are many scenarios that can result in a rider falling from a horse. Examples of situations that may result in a rider falling include the following:

- horse bucks a rider off,
- horse balks at a jumps obstacle,
- horse rears and rider is dislodged,
- horse changes direction suddenly,
- horse stumbles, trips, or breaks down,
- horse tosses or dips its head suddenly,
- horse is spooked and takes off suddenly,
- horse collides with another horse or object,
- horse takes off or lands poorly when jumping,
- rider becomes unseated or loses their balance,
- horse clips the heels of another horse when racing,
- horse is travelling at speed and slows down suddenly,
- horse hits a jumps obstacle and goes into a rotational fall,
- rider's foot comes out of a stirrup and they lose their balance.

It is useful to condense these situations into typical fall scenarios. When considering fall safety training techniques, the main concern is the way in which a rider is likely to impact the ground, and the subsequent forces of impact if landing at speed. It is important that the training techniques be designed to mitigate injury in situations where the rider is travelling at significant speed at the time of impact with the ground.

Because the direction of travel is forward when riding, the rider in most cases will be falling forward or sideways if travelling at speed. It is important that riders are trained to initially respond in a way that reduces the risk of blunt force impact to the head and spine. Blunt force trauma occurs as a result of a large amount of force being applied over a short period of time, often as a result of impact with the ground. With proper training in fall safety techniques, riders will also be better prepared to negotiate the significant forces of angular momentum as a result of being flipped or rotated after the point of initial impact with the ground. A tuck position following impact with the ground at speed is imperative to reduce injury risk.

Fall Safety Skills

The following is a summary of the fall safety skills that are important for mitigating the risk of injury in various fall modes and reducing the risk of crush or trample injury. Riders often have a tendency to hold onto the reins in a fall and this increases the risk of dangerous consequences (Medical Equestrian Association, 2012). Letting go of the reins is not an intuitive thing for riders to do. It is important that riders practice activities to let go of the reins in fall safety training—so it becomes encoded into their memory banks as the first part of the emergency response in a fall.

FEET-FIRST LANDING POSITION

Feet-first landing, when not landing at speed, is straightforward. It is important to develop good feet-first landing habits to minimise the risk of soft tissue injury such as ankle sprain, knee injury or stress injury to the back. Riders will dismount their horse many times and may often land on hard or uneven surfaces, which can result in sprains and strains.

If landing feet-first at speed, riders will be flipped or rotated following impact with the ground. Good feet-first landing habits should be developed so the rider does not have to consciously think about their landing position in a fall at speed. By developing the habit of landing with the arms in the brace position with good knee bend, riders will be well positioned to tuck-and-roll if necessary.

PRONE LANDING DIRECTION

When a galloping horse slows suddenly, stumbles or trips, the rider's momentum will continue, resulting in a forward fall to the ground. In this situation, riders who are untrained in fall safety skills may have a tendency to allow their body to go from a favourable riding position (being semi-tucked) to an unfavourable, open-body position—landing prone. A rider in this position on impact with the ground will increase their risk of serious injury such as blunt force impact to the head, and of spinal injury as a result of being flipped or rotated at speed.

Riders should maintain muscle tension so they stay in a semi-tucked (or riding position) and use a 4-point landing technique if coming down in a prone direction. The initial vertical impact force can then be absorbed by the arms and legs (as opposed to the torso or head).

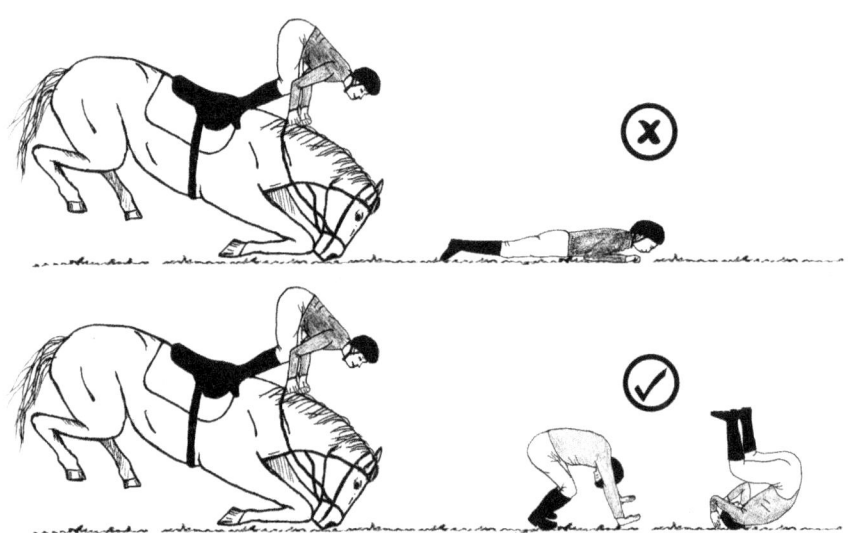

Most importantly, a 4-point landing position will enable the rider to continue into a tuck-and-roll, after the initial impact with the ground, without having to change their body shape. This will reduce the risk of head and spinal injury when landing at speed.

SIDEWAYS FALL

Riders routinely dismount from the side of their horse and coming off sideways is also a common fall scenario. This may explain why, in a sideways fall, riders may have a tendency to hang onto the reins. In many sideways falls, the rider may end up falling in a 'spread eagle' position or with arms and legs flailing once they become dislodged or are thrown from their horse. When falling sideways, the rider should let go of the reins, quickly move their arms into the brace position and try to get into a more closed body position before impacting the ground. This will assist in rolling clear of the horse and reduce the risk of crush injury or getting dragged under the horse. If landing feet-first, it is likely that the rider will be forced to roll—forward, sideways, or backward—after they land. If landing in a prone direction, the rider can break their fall in a 4-point landing position, then tuck-and-roll.

HORSE REARS

When a horse rears significantly, the rider may tend to do one of three things: hang onto the reins as they lose balance and try to stay on their horse; grasp the horse's mane or neck to remain on the horse and to assist the horse to come back down; or do an emergency dismount. Pulling on the reins is a high-risk situation that will increase the possibility of the horse falling backward together with the rider. Grasping the horse's mane or neck will assist the rider to stay on the horse, but it also carries a risk of crush injury if the horse should continue to rear and then fall. If the rider attempts to remain on a horse that rears significantly and the horse ends up falling, both horse and rider will be falling together, making it difficult for the rider to land or fall clear of the horse.

The safest option is an emergency dismount from a horse that rears significantly (without trying to evaluate the circumstances of whether the horse is likely to fall or not). After dismounting, the rider should quickly move clear and distance themself from the horse.

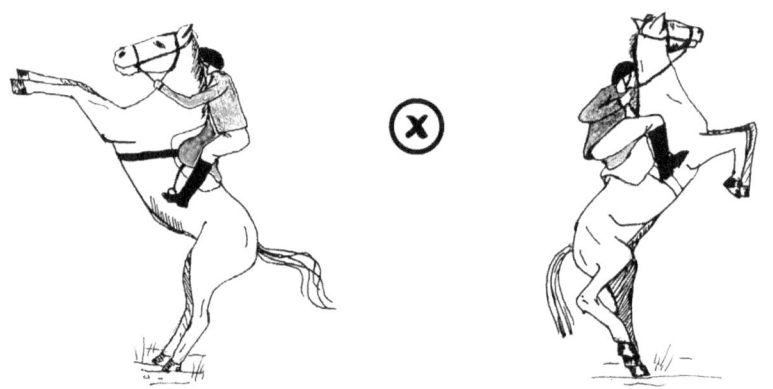

Hanging on to a horse that rears significantly increases the risk of crush injury.

When a horse rears, the safest option is to do an emergency dismount (to the side of the horse if possible) and then quickly move away from the horse.

FORWARD DIVE

When a horse trips, breaks down, is in a rotational fall, or lands poorly after a jump, the rider may often be in a position where they are falling forward, head-first, in a vertical or near vertical position. The safest response in this scenario is to quickly let go of the reins and move the arms into the brace position (with muscle tension in the arms), to protect the head and neck from a direct impact with the ground, and then tuck-and-roll.

BACKWARD LANDING—BACKWARD FEET-FIRST

The legs can absorb the initial force of impact, and the rider should quickly move their arms into the brace position. After the initial landing, the rider should maintain a tuck position and *not resist being flipped or rotated*, and continue into a backward roll, swinging the arms backward (over their head) to reduce the force of impact on the head and neck.

BACKWARD LANDING—BACKWARD, NOT FEET-FIRST

Where a rider is falling backward without being in a position to break the initial impact of the fall feet-first, the best way of mitigating injury is to be in a tucked position with arms in the brace position to provide some protection for the head and neck. In a tuck position, the impact forces may be partially absorbed by muscle tension and, if landing at speed, this is likely to reduce the level of subsequent trauma to the head and neck.

BEING FLIPPED OR SOMERSAULTED IN THE AIR

This type of fall is likely to result in a loss of visual orientation with the rider not knowing where the ground is. When, for example, a gymnast or diver is somersaulting, their focus changes from visual orientation to kinaesthetic orientation. Kinaesthetic orientation means awareness of your body position when in the air even though you cannot see where the ground is.

Lindsay Nylund—1978 Commonwealth Games—double somersault with full turn

Fall safety training in somersaulting skills will improve kinaesthetic awareness and develop skills to better respond when being somersaulted. This is a more advanced skill that requires more practice than other basic skills. If the rider is somersaulted, there is still a possibility that orientation will be lost despite having done some training. In this situation, the safest response is to maintain muscle tension with the body tucked and the arms in the brace position until impact with the ground. This provides the greatest level of protection for the head and neck when orientation is lost. It is important to not look up and extend the head and neck to try to see where the ground is—there will generally not be enough time to regain orientation before impacting the ground.

ROTATIONAL FALLS AND LANDING AT SPEED

In a rotational fall and/or when landing at speed riders must not only deal with the vertical impact force, but also the subsequent forces as a result of horizontal speed. The best way to mitigate risk of injury in these situations is to let go of the reins, quickly get the arms into the brace position to protect the head and neck from the initial vertical impact force and continue into a tuck-and-roll so the rider's horizontal momentum continues after the initial landing. This will reduce blunt force impact to the head, neck or other parts of the body and also decrease the risk of getting crushed by a falling horse.

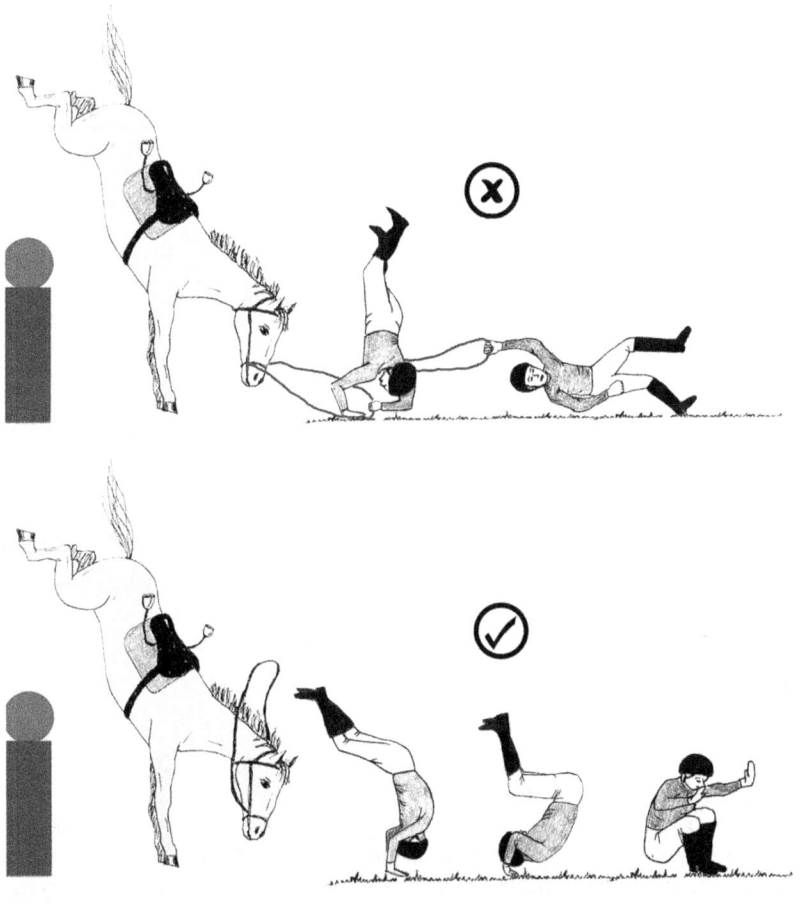

The brace position followed by tuck-and-roll reduces the risk of injury to the head and neck and assists the rider to roll clear of a falling horse.

Reducing the Risk of Crush and Trample Injury

CRUSH INJURY

The greatest risk of crush injury is where the rider and horse are falling together and the rider is underneath or very close to the horse on impact with the ground. The risk of crush injury can be reduced by letting go of the reins and quickly moving the arms into the brace position as soon as the rider realises that they or their horse are falling. On impact with the ground, the rider should try to maintain a tuck position in order to roll clear of the horse. The skill of letting go of the reins and quickly putting the arms in the brace position, followed by tuck-and-roll can be developed and improved with training.

A horse may rear suddenly and may or may not fall. Because the rider may not have time to consciously evaluate the circumstances to determine if the horse will or will not recover itself, the safest option when a horse rears significantly is to do an emergency dismount, then quickly move clear (if landing feet-first) or land, tuck-and-roll (if the rider is falling when they land). Trying to stay on a horse that rears significantly increases the risk of crush injury.

After repeating the emergency response drill of letting go of the reins and quickly moving the arms into the brace position (with many repetitions over a number of training sessions), riders will normally find that the movement sequence becomes a more intuitive response—triggered by a single conscious decision to react in an emergency.

Because letting go of the reins is not a natural action for riders, some riders may only be able to do this in an emergency through practice. Once free of the horse, the rider can better control their body shape, their landing position, and tuck-and-roll to preserve their horizontal momentum if falling or landing at speed. Furthermore, if a rider is in the unfortunate position of ending up underneath a falling horse, a tuck position (with muscle tension) is anatomically more favourable to protect against serious injury. Serious crush injury is often caused by trauma to the torso or abdominal area, and this can be mitigated if a rider is in a tuck position.

TRAMPLE INJURY

The same emergency response action—let go of the reins, move the arms quickly into the brace position, followed by tuck-and-roll—is also the best method of reducing the risk of trample injury. Trample injury can occur as a result of the rider hanging onto the reins in a fall and getting dragged under their horse, or as a result of other horses in close proximity being unable to avoid a fallen rider. In a tuck position, riders can better maintain their forward momentum, giving trailing horses and riders slightly more time to change direction and possibly avoid the fallen rider when travelling at speed.

Furthermore, if a rider is trampled or kicked, a tuck position is anatomically better than an open body position to reduce the risk of serious injury.

Biomechanics and Forces of Impact

Riders must negotiate vertical forces of impact when coming down from a height and horizontal forces when travelling at speed. These include angular momentum (being flipped or forced to roll) and centrifugal forces. There are some basic principles of physics that can help us to understand these forces and the best way of mitigating injury.

Newton's First Law of Motion

A body at rest will remain at rest or a body in motion will remain in motion unless acted on by an external force.

This law of physics has important implications for the rider when coming down from a height and also from a horse that is moving. In simple terms, this law of physics means that if we are falling or travelling at speed (the motion part), a force must be applied to stop the rider's motion. The resultant forces to bring the rider to rest include impact with the ground and sometimes also impact with other things such as railings, obstacles and/or horse(s). The techniques that are used to break the vertical force of impact with the ground are essentially the same, whether coming down from a stationary horse or coming down from a horse that is moving.

The additional issue when landing from a moving horse is that the rider will generally be flipped or forced to roll (angular momentum) as a result of their horizontal velocity at the time of impact with the ground. As a result, the rider must also deal with forces of rotation when falling from a moving horse. The faster the horse is moving, the greater these forces will be.

Newton's Second Law of Motion

The force on a body is equal to its mass times acceleration (or deceleration).

$$F = M \times A$$

When coming down from a height or at speed, the amount of force that a rider must deal with is proportional to the rate of deceleration—in other words, how quickly the rider's momentum stops. In order to reduce the forces of impact, riders should try to position themselves so they do not come to an abrupt halt. This is the benefit of tuck-and-roll when landing at speed—it means that the deceleration takes place over a longer period of time.

The acceleration or deceleration (A) is equal to how quickly velocity changes:

$$A = \frac{\text{Change in Velocity}}{\text{Time}}$$

If the time to come to rest increases, then the deceleration (A) decreases. Increasing the time taken to come to rest will substantially reduce the impact forces when landing or falling.

Force of Impact in a Vertical Landing or Fall Position

In a vertical landing, the velocity on impact with the ground is a result of the height that the rider is coming down from—a function of gravity. The time taken to come to rest on impact with the ground is proportional to the distance travelled before stopping (the stopping distance). We can use the following formula to calculate the vertical impact force if we know the stopping distance but not the time taken to come to rest:

$$F = \frac{M \times G \times H}{D}$$

where   F = force of impact (newtons)
M = rider mass (kg)
G = gravity = 9.8 (m/s²)
H = height of dismount or fall (m)
D = stopping distance (m)

The force of impact (F) in various situations can be calculated. The following are examples of the vertical impact forces when dismounting or falling from a 1.5 m (5 ft) height. These examples illustrate the importance of good landing technique.

FEET-FIRST LANDING—POOR TECHNIQUE

Rider mass = 50 kg (110 lbs)
Distance = 1.5 m (5 ft)

Stopping distance = 20 cm (8 in)
Poor knee bend

$$\text{Force of impact} = \frac{50 \times 9.8 \times 1.5}{0.2} = 3{,}675 \text{ newtons}$$

9.8 newtons of force is equivalent to approximately 1 kg in weight, so a 50 kg (110 lb) rider resists a force of 490 newtons (9.8 × 50) when standing. In the above example, with poor landing technique, the rider must temporarily absorb 7.5 times body weight (3,675 / 490).

FEET-FIRST LANDING—GOOD TECHNIQUE

Rider mass = 50 kg (110 lbs)
Distance = 1.5 m (5 ft)

Stopping distance = 40 cm (16 in)

Good knee bend

$$\text{Force of impact} = \frac{50 \times 9.8 \times 1.5}{0.4} = 1{,}838 \text{ newtons}$$

With good landing technique, using a more absorbent knee bend, a 50 kg (110 lb) rider must temporarily absorb 3.75 times body weight (1,838 / 490). The better landing technique in the above example results in a 50 per cent reduction in impact force.

Poor feet-first landing technique is unlikely to result in a serious injury—possibly just strained muscles or excessive wear and tear over time. However, when a rider comes down head-first, the difference between good and poor technique can be critical. The impact forces when landing head-first from the same height, 1.5 m (5 ft), with nothing other than helmet and turf to absorb the impact, are significant. This situation may occur if a rider hangs onto the reins and unexpectedly impacts the ground head-first. The stopping distance may only be about 7 cm (3 in)—say 5 cm (2 in) give if landing on a turf surface and about 2 cm (1 in) impact absorption from the helmet.

DIRECT HEAD-FIRST IMPACT (TURF SURFACE)

Very small stopping distance = 7cm (3 in)

$$\text{Force of impact} = \frac{50 \times 9.8 \times 1.5}{0.07} = 10{,}500 \text{ newtons}$$

Mertz et al. (2003) reported that the fracture tolerance value for peak loading of the upper neck for compression force is likely to be about 4,000 newtons for an average adult. In a direct head-first impact from a height of 1.5 m (5 ft) with nothing other than helmet and turf for protection, the 10,500 newton vertical impact force would likely result in a serious compression fracture of the upper cervical vertebrae.

HEAD-FIRST FALL WITH ARMS IN THE BRACE POSITION (TURF SURFACE)

Stopping distance = 30 cm (12 in): arms plus 7 cm (3 in): turf and helmet

The relative strength of the major muscle groups in the arms is approximately 50 per cent of the relative strength of the muscle groups in the legs (Corbin et al., 2014). If a rider can land feet-first from a height of 1.5 m (5 ft) with a stopping distance of approximately 30 cm (12 in), then they should be capable of stopping half (50 per cent) of the downward velocity from the same height with their arms.

The velocity when impacting the ground from a height of 1.5 m (5 ft) is 5.4 metres per second (12 mph). If 50 per cent of the downward velocity were stopped by the arm muscles tensed in the brace position, then the velocity at the point of head impact would be halved to 2.7 metres per second (6 mph). This is equivalent to a direct head-first impact from a height of 37 cm (15 in). The remaining compression force on the head and neck, with the same 7 cm (3 in) stopping distance, 5 cm (2 in) give in the turf + 2 cm (1 in) impact absorption from the helmet, can be calculated as follows:

$$\text{Force of impact} = \frac{50 \times 9.8 \times 0.37}{0.07} = 2{,}590 \text{ newtons}$$

Riders who have learned to let go of the reins and quickly move their arms into the brace position using arm muscles to protect their head and neck can significantly reduce the risk of catastrophic and serious injury. In the above example, of good technique, the vertical force of impact with the ground is reduced by 75 per cent (2,590 / 10,500). The force of impact with arms in brace position may still result in an injury; however, it would be unlikely to be catastrophic in this scenario—where the upper neck has an approximate fracture tolerance of 4,000 newtons for compression force.

Forces of Impact when Landing at Speed

When landing at speed, a rider will be flipped or forced to roll. Most people who are untrained in rolling techniques are likely to be very anxious in this situation. A natural untrained reaction may be to try to resist being flipped or rotated, by going into an open body position (to resist the forces of rotation) or by using the arms to try to stop momentum, or alternatively, by relaxing and going limp. These untrained response actions will substantially increase the risk of injury when landing at speed. Though it may seem counter-intuitive, riders need to do everything they can to allow their momentum to continue (Newton's first law of motion). On impacting the ground at speed, irrespective of landing direction, riders should quickly move into a tight tuck-and-roll position to preserve their momentum as much as possible. This will ensure that they come to rest over a longer period of time and minimise the magnitude of blunt force impact on any body part.

Good rolling technique includes:

- arms in the brace position with muscle tension to provide some protection for the head and neck,
- head tucked in with chin close to the chest,
- hip and abdominal muscles flexed, and
- back rounded to facilitate a smooth rolling technique.

There will also be significant centrifugal forces on the rider when rolling at speed. If the rider allows themselves to go limp or relax, these forces tend to pull them into an open body position, resulting in significant blunt force impact to any body part that becomes exposed when tumbling at speed. The rider must use all of their available strength and muscle tension to stay in a tucked position so they continue to roll for as long as possible. This includes keeping the muscles in the neck tight to ensure that the chin is kept close to the chest and tightening abdominal and hip flexor muscles as well as maintaining strong arm muscles—in the brace position.

When rolling at speed, riders will become disoriented. *The rider should not look up and try to regain their orientation before coming completely to rest.*

Physical conditioning exercises for the neck, arms, abdominal, and hip flexor muscles will assist the rider to maintain good body shape in a fall when needing to tuck-and-roll. These are detailed in the section 'Warm-up and Physical Conditioning Exercises'. Riders of any age and fitness level can do these exercises which will assist in improving riding fitness and also provide some protection from injury in a fall.

When tumbling at speed, it is preferable that the rider rolls end-over-end many times in a high-speed fall before coming to rest—this should not be resisted. Riders may also be tempted to jump up quickly as their momentum slows. This temptation should also be resisted for the following reasons:

- The sensation of slowing down is relative to the initial speed of travel. Coming out of the tuck position prematurely (while still rolling) can result in a significant unexpected blunt force impact to the head, neck, or other parts of the body.
- There may still be horses nearby or following and the rider may be hit or trampled by these horses.
- If there is a risk of being trampled or impacted by a falling horse, it is anatomically more favourable to be in a tuck position with strong muscle tension.

After coming to rest, the rider should maintain their tuck position and 'count to three' until it is clear that there are no horses coming. The rider should then relax, breathe, and try to evaluate their condition before getting up.

Simulation, Skills Transfer, and Retention

Simulation Activities

Simulation activities are a great way to train and prepare for emergency situations. There are many situations where people cannot be trained in a real scenario and simulations can provide the best and safest method of preparation for these situations.

Examples of simulation activities:

- dummies or mannequins used to learn cardiopulmonary resuscitation techniques,
- flight simulators for pilots to develop emergency-response skills, and
- mechanical horses used to develop riding skills and fitness.

Simulations can be very simple, such as body-shaping exercises to develop coordination and muscle conditioning, or simple drills to learn part of a movement sequence.

PRACTICE LETTING GO OF THE REINS IN AN EMERGENCY

BODY-SHAPING EXERCISE TO LEARN PART OF THE DIVE ROLL TECHNIQUE

60 cm (2 ft) high block.

Simulations can also include more sophisticated equipment or advanced training.

MECHANICAL HORSE—SIDEWAYS/BACKWARD FALL SIMULATION EXERCISE

BICYCLE SIMULATION EXERCISE—FORWARD DIVE AT SPEED

MECHANICAL HORSE SIMULATION EXERCISE—FORWARD DIVE AT SPEED

Simulation activities should be designed so that they

- can be learned and practiced safely,
- gradually progress skill level,
- develop muscle conditioning,
- match real scenarios as closely as possible, and
- are carried out in a similar environment to the real scenario.

ENVIRONMENTAL SIMULATION

When practicing or learning a skill, the movement sequence consolidates a path into the brain and, if practiced often enough, can be performed intuitively. This is called memory encoding and is a powerful tool that can enable very quick response action in an emergency.

For example, when fleeing danger, we only need to make a single conscious decision to run and our unconscious brain does the rest—we do not need to consciously think of all the muscle actions and movement sequences required to run.

Environmental variables are encoded and stored together with a learned skill. To maximise skills transfer, riders should do some training sessions in circumstances that are as close as possible to their riding environment. Examples of environmental simulation include:

- jockeys and track-work riders—practice on or adjacent to a race track or training track,
- jumps jockeys—practice jumping over and adjacent to a hurdle,
- showjumping or cross-country riders—practice jumping over and adjacent to a jumps obstacle,
- polo and polocrosse players—practice on or near a competition or practice field.

While the skills can be learned and practiced from any location, including indoors in a gym, doing some sessions in an environment that is the same as or similar to the horse riding location will facilitate skills transfer and a more intuitive response action in an emergency. Equipment such as a replica horse and mechanical horse can also be used for environmental simulation activities.

The goal of the training is to enable the rider, on recognition that they are falling, to make a single conscious decision to react, with the rest of the movement sequence—letting go of the reins, the brace position, land, tuck-and-roll—being performed intuitively.

DRESS REHEARSAL

Dress rehearsal is an important final stage in the preparation for many competitive and high-performance activities, including sports, games, theatre, music, military training, and a range of other activities.

This is another means of minimising the difference between training and competition or real-world experiences. For example, in a lifesaving course, fully clothed swimmers can be trained to rescue each other to simulate a real emergency situation.

It is recommended that riders learn basic fall safety skills initially with comfortable non-restrictive clothing, such as shorts and T-shirt, tracksuit, or riding clothes such as jodhpurs. Once the basic skills have been learned properly, it is recommended that some subsequent training sessions be completed wearing riding gear such as:

- riding uniform,
- helmet,
- body protector/vest (if one is worn while riding), and
- holding and releasing equipment such as reins, whip, polo mallet, or polocrosse racket.

As well as letting go of the reins in a fall, riders should do some practice to let go of any other equipment that they may be holding so their landing and tumbling skill will not be impeded in a fall.

IMPORTANT SAFETY NOTE

Safety equipment such as helmet and body protector should not impede a rider's ability to perform the skills. When performing skills for the first time with helmet and body protector, riders should repeat the basics and skill progression activities before performing more difficult skills. These include basics such as body shaping, rock and roll, and forward roll. If safety equipment impedes the rider from performing the basic skills correctly, then they should not progress to more advanced skills and need to consider options such as wearing a less restrictive body protector. For some riders it may simply be a matter of becoming accustomed to performing the skills wearing their riding gear. Work with your qualified instructor to progress safely.

Skills Transfer

There will always be differences between simulations and real scenarios. The goal of simulation is to model and develop skills that approximate a real situation, without taking any significant risks or compromising safety. Once a skill has been learned so that it can be performed consistently well without hesitation, then in an emergency situation it is most likely that the rider will be capable of carrying out the learned response if required.

The manner in which knowledge and skills are stored in the brain and retrieved is complex and beyond the scope of this book. However, it is well accepted by psychologists that well-designed simulation activities can be of benefit in preparing for real scenarios.

Practicing skills in a variety of ways and in different environments, providing the practice is not significantly different from a real situation, will enable better skill transfer in an emergency. Consider the following example:

A rider under supervision of a qualified instructor, successfully learns a basic dive roll technique from a standing position onto a soft landing surface, and then, over a number of training sessions, progresses their skill level as follows:

- dive roll to a harder landing surface,
- dive roll from a run,
- dive roll from increased height,
- dive roll over a foam vaulting box,
- dive roll over a jumps obstacle,
- dive roll adjacent to or over a replica horse, and
- dive roll with equipment in hand and releasing the equipment when in the air.

The rider is essentially performing the same skill over and over again, and each time there is a progression, the brain will link or form an association between the situation and the skill—a dive roll. In a head-first fall, once the rider recognises they are falling and lets go of the reins, they are likely to perform a dive roll without much conscious thought, having previously performed this skill in a variety of situations.

Variations on performing the skills are beneficial because these experiences will allow the formation of multiple *neural pathways* to retrieve what is essentially the same skill. This is the benefit of environmental simulation—memory encoding of environmental variables.

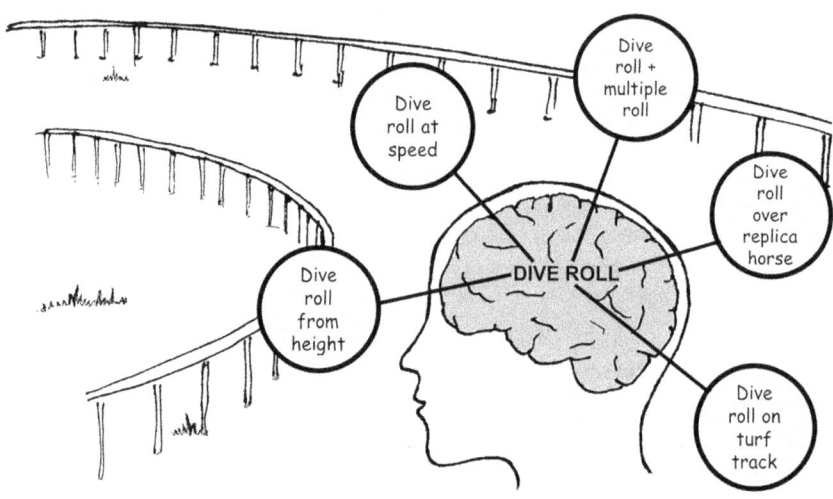

Because riders are not able to practice fall safety techniques in real fall scenarios, it is important that fall safety training provides a variety of activities to enhance the transfer of skills to real scenarios (Newell et al., 1976).

Skill Retention

A number of factors can influence how well skills are retained over time. Basic skills that are repeated more often will be retained longer than complex skills that are repeated less often. Methods of improving skill retention include:

- pre-ride safety routines (taking only a few minutes before riding each day),
- periodic refresher training (yearly or six-monthly),
- physical conditioning exercises to maintain fitness and muscle memory, and
- overlearning (spaced repetition of a skill after it has been initially mastered).

Periodic refresher training will significantly enhance skill retention as a result of overlearning (Melnick, 1971). A literature review titled 'Retention and Transfer of Motor Skills' also noted that overlearning—repetition beyond what is required for initial skill mastery—significantly enhances retention (Fischman et al., 1982). This also highlights the importance of doing a pre-ride safety routine to repeatedly practice and refine some basic techniques.

Fall Safety Technique Analysis

The initial emergency response, once the rider recognises that they are falling, is the same for all falls. The benefits of a single emergency action are significant for riders:

- Only a single conscious decision needs to be made to respond. There is no need to evaluate the circumstances and choose between various courses of action.
- The initial movement sequence, with training, can be performed by most riders very quickly—within half a second (500 ms) of recognition of falling.
- After a few training sessions and many repetitions, the movement sequence will start to become intuitive once the rider decides to let go of the reins.
- The brace position will provide protection for the head and neck.
- Letting go of the reins will reduce risk of the rider getting dragged under their horse.
- Letting go of the reins will reduce risk of getting crushed by a falling horse.
- Once free of the horse, the rider can control their body shape, land, tuck-and-roll.

BRACE!

⇒ (L) Let go of reins — (B) Brace position

↘ (L) Land — (T) Tuck-and-roll ⇒

ROLL!

Often a fall will be preceded by some issue or warning sign that can alert the rider to the risk. Warning signals may include becoming unbalanced, a foot coming out of the stirrup, a jockey in proximity being in trouble or falling. In some situations, the problem may be averted or the horse may recover itself. No changes need to be made to riding skills or practices in order to learn and apply fall safety skills. The benefit of being alerted to a risk is that the rider can, while trying to recover (or allowing their horse to recover), be poised ready to take emergency action the instant it becomes obvious that a fall is inevitable.

The realisation of a fall becoming inevitable may include a horse continuing to fall or break down, the rider becoming unseated to a point that they cannot recover, or the rider flying through the air. As soon as the rider realises that they are falling, emergency response action should be commenced without hesitation and without trying to evaluate the circumstances.

LET GO OF THE REINS AND QUICKLY GET THE ARMS INTO THE BRACE POSITION

- The arms should form a barrier around the head and neck with muscle tension.
- Body shape should remain in riding position (semi-tucked), abdominal and hip flexor muscles should be tightened—do not allow body shape to be stretched out or relaxed.
- If orientation is lost (not knowing where the ground is), the head should be tucked in between the arms and the rider should not lift their head up to try to spot where the ground is.
- Once visual orientation is lost, it generally cannot be regained in the time available before impact with the ground—head-first landing direction must be the assumed landing direction.

With the arms in the brace position (with strong muscle tension) and body tucked, the rider is in a very favourable position to divert forces of impact away from the head and neck. The initial emergency response for all fall scenarios can, with practice, become intuitive and this will enable riders to respond very quickly when a fall becomes inevitable.

LAND, TUCK-AND-ROLL

Following the initial landing, in most situations where the horse is moving, the rider will be flipped or rotated. On impact with the ground riders should maintain a tight tuck position and roll without resisting the momentum.

No attempt should be made to come out of the tuck position or stop the momentum, or to try and regain orientation by looking or standing up before coming to complete rest. In a high-speed fall when rolling at speed, orientation will generally be lost. After tumbling at speed, a rider might think they have come to rest, when in fact they are still rolling. This is simply a case of our sensory nerves (called proprioceptors) being temporarily confused or subdued by the centrifugal force of rolling.

A good way of understanding this phenomenon is to think of driving a car at speed on a freeway and then slowing down to take an exit at a speed of, say 60 km/h (40 mph). This seems like a snail's pace after travelling at 100 km/h (60 mph) or more for a while. But if we were to try to turn a 90-degree corner at 60 km/h (40 mph), we would quickly realise that we are in fact still travelling fast and that our sensation of travelling slowly is an illusion created by the relative change in speed.

A track-work rider once explained that after falling off his horse and rolling multiple times at speed, he prematurely stood up (a natural tendency) only to fall again and suffer a significant impact to his head and subsequent concussion—he had in fact not yet come to rest.

After coming to a perceived rest, riders should:

- maintain a tight tuck position with strong muscle tension;
- count to three (one, and, two, and three);
- listen to hear if there may be a horse or horses still in proximity—and if so, start the count again; and
- when the coast is clear, relax, breathe, and then evaluate condition before standing up.

This fall safety technique can be applied in all fall scenarios and, with practice, should become intuitive, enabling riders to respond very quickly when a fall becomes inevitable.

LANDING TECHNIQUES

Depending on the fall scenario, with practice, riders can learn to execute various landing techniques to further mitigate the risk of impact injury. A rider's ability to execute various landing techniques on initial impact with the ground will depend on factors such as the time available in the fall, whether or not the rider has lost orientation when travelling through the air, and the rider's aptitude and skill level in learning aerial and tumbling skills. Irrespective of these factors and riders' ability to learn aerial and tumbling skills, the initial emergency response and the subsequent tuck-and-roll after impacting the ground remain unchanged.

Riders should learn and practice a variety of landing and tumbling techniques, to enable them to respond more intuitively when impacting the ground. Some of the techniques are relatively simple, such as feet-first landing followed by a roll. Some will require more practice, such as 4-point landing (feet and hands impacting the ground at the same time). And some are more advanced, such as dive roll from height and/or at speed. Riders should not be deterred from doing fall safety training due to inability to learn the more advanced techniques. Learning the basics will afford considerably more protection in a fall than being untrained.

Superman and Superwoman

Life takes us on a journey that we cannot always foresee. But the lessons from these journeys can be passed on for the benefit of all. The following are the fall experiences of two great people who have lived through significant adversity.

SUPERMAN

Christopher Reeve, an experienced eventing competitor, had a serious cross-country fall in 1995.

Reeve's horse made a refusal at a jump. Witnesses said that the horse began the third fence jump and suddenly stopped. Reeve fell forward off the horse, holding on to the reins. His hands somehow became tangled in the reins and the bridle and bit were pulled off the horse. He landed head-first on the far side of the fence, shattering his first and second vertebrae. This spinal injury paralysed him from the neck down (Romano, 1995).

SUPERWOMAN

Michelle Payne, after her historic victory in the 2015 Melbourne Cup, fell from her horse in a country race in 2016 in Mildura, Australia.

'I remember falling and I remember thinking I held on too long ... I was too far gone and around the horse's neck, which put me in a position to fall underneath her and she did run over me', Payne said. Her horse stepped on her after she fell, splitting her pancreas. The surgeon saved three quarters of the severed organ, sewing it to her stomach (ABC News, 2016).

There is little time for evaluation of circumstances or conscious deliberation in a fall. Once a fall becomes *inevitable*, riders should immediately let go of the reins and quickly put their arms in the brace position to protect their head and neck, and then tuck-and-roll on impact with the ground. With some practice, this can be performed as a spontaneous response within half a second. It is the odds-on response action in a fall.

SKILL LEARNING AND TRAINING METHODS

The more I practice, the luckier I get.

—Gary Player
Three-time British Open Golf Champion

Warm-up and Conditioning Exercises | Safe to do unsupervised |

It is widely accepted that a warm-up is beneficial and important for all sporting and physical activities, whether recreational, competitive, or high performance.

Most riders will have no hesitation in doing warm-up activities for their horse, but many riders may not do any general warm-up activity themselves and rely on the initial riding activity as their only means of warm-up. Not only will general warm-up activities provide safety benefits by reducing the risk of injury; they will also improve riding performance.

Riders should develop the good habit of doing a warm-up routine before each riding session on any day. The benefits of doing general warm-up activities are significant and include

- improved circulation,
- improved muscle conditioning,
- better retention of fall safety skills,
- improved balance and mental readiness, and
- improved flexibility and reduced risk of muscle strain.

All riders should do general warm-up activities before getting on their horse each day. The warm-up routine should be developed based on the rider's age, skill, fitness level, and the nature of their riding activity. The suggested activities that follow provide some general guidelines and can be adapted to suit each rider's circumstances.

The amount of time that should be allocated to general warm-up activities independent of horse riding activity will depend on individual circumstances and the goals of the riding session. A general pre-ride warm-up may take as little as five minutes for recreational riders and up to thirty minutes for competitive and high-performance riders. Even a ten or fifteen minute warm-up program can provide a significant benefit to high-performance riders who are not currently doing any general warm-up activities.

Five Elements for Pre-ride Warm-up

The warm-up routine should include activities from each of the following groups:

1. cardiovascular
2. joint mobilisation
3. flexibility exercises
4. muscle conditioning
5. pre-ride safety routine

Some examples of warm-up activities in each group follow. It is not necessary to include all of the suggested activities because many of the exercises overlap. Choose the ones that are most suitable and include other activities that are not listed if required. If time is limited, doing a couple of minutes on each group activity is much better than doing no warm-up at all.

The general warm-up should be done before commencing any horse riding activity. It is best carried out on a grassed area with an exercise mat approximately 180 × 120 cm (4 × 6 ft). The warm-up routine should ideally be done at the riding venue or alternatively at home or at a local park—anywhere where there is some grass or a suitable surface.

1. CARDIOVASCULAR

Jogging or running: In cold weather, it will be beneficial to wear warm clothing (such as a tracksuit) and allocate more time to cardio activities than in hot weather. In hot weather, one or two minutes cardio activity should be adequate. If space is limited, jogging or jumping activities on the spot can be substituted.

Examples of jumping activities: straight jump, star jump, tuck jump:

2. JOINT MOBILISATION

Joint mobilisation should be done through a full range of motion to maintain joint flexibility. It is important not to be too aggressive or bounce to avoid soft tissue strain. Activities include circling or gentle rotation of the wrists, shoulders, back, hips, and knees.

Shoulder and back mobilisation exercise

3. FLEXIBILITY EXERCISES

This is an important part of all warm-up routines to minimise the risk of muscle strain and to support skills development. Do stretching exercises after cardio activities and, in colder weather, wear warmer clothing. Be sure to stretch muscles equally on both sides to avoid muscle imbalance. Repeat stretching exercises two or three times, and hold for ten to twenty seconds. Bouncing should generally be avoided.

Legs:

Hamstring stretch

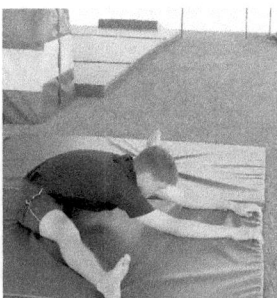
Pancake (hamstrings and adductors)

Forward lunge (hip flexors)

Upper body:

Deltoid stretch   Pectoral stretch   Oblique (side) stretch

4. MUSCLE CONDITIONING

Sporting activities tend to build muscles and muscle groups that are specific to the particular activity. Riders will tend to develop strength and endurance particularly of muscles in their legs (quadriceps and adductor muscles), and abdominal and back muscles. Most riders will not tend to develop strength in their arms as a result of riding activity. It is highly recommended that riders include the following arm-conditioning exercise in their warm-up or fitness program to support fall safety skills.

Arms: Push-ups from 4-point landing position—gently touch the head on the grass/mat during each push-up. The body position should remain rigid so only the arms are working.

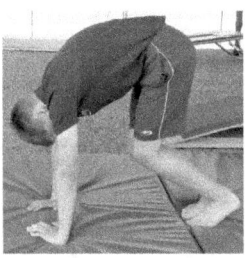 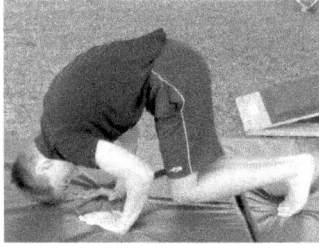 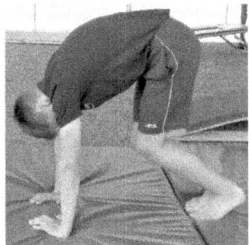

Abdominal and hip flexors: Open tuck rocks—maintain rigid body shape and just move the arms to rock:

A good strategy for any sporting activity is to do some physical conditioning exercises for the opposing (called antagonistic) muscle groups. This will improve joint stability, skeletal alignment, and also minimise 'wear and tear' as a result of continual loading being placed on certain areas of the body. As well as exercises to warm-up for riding activity, exercises for other muscle groups can be included as a means of injury prevention. Consult your medical practitioner or fitness instructor for exercises that will assist in recovery from injury and for injury prevention.

NECK EXERCISES

Neck-conditioning exercises are very important for riders. Even in a relatively minor fall—such as where the rider lands feet-first at an angle and may roll awkwardly—there can be some force applied to the head and neck. A small increase in muscle strength in the neck muscles can assist in reducing the risk of neck injury in both minor and more serious falls by providing some additional support for the cervical vertebrae.

It is recommended that riders do a brief pre-ride safety routine before each day's riding activity, and the first element of this routine is neck exercises.

When doing the neck exercises, move through the full range of joint motion. The first two exercises are for flexibility and mobilisation, to be done as stretches rather than muscle conditioning:

Lateral flexion—side-to-side   Forward and backward

Next, do the following exercises with resistance, slowly moving the head for five seconds in each direction while applying resistance with the hands. Repeat a second time with increased resistance (but not to the point of experiencing any pain).

- lateral flexion with resistance—left and right (five seconds in each direction)
- backward extension and forward flexion with resistance (five seconds in each direction)

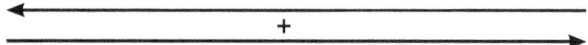

Five seconds moving the head to the right + five seconds moving the head to the left

Five seconds moving the head to the left + five seconds moving the head to the right

Five seconds moving the head backward + five seconds moving the head forward

Five seconds moving the head backward + five seconds moving the head forward

Repeat the neck resistance exercises a second time. Remember to exercise through the full range of motion. The neck exercise routine will take about two minutes.

Skill learning and training methods

5. PRE-RIDE SAFETY ROUTINE

This is the most important element of the pre-ride warm-up and will assist in the retention of fall safety skills that have been previously learned. The routine should be completed twice, with a short break between each routine if desired. The pre-ride safety routine should be varied periodically and only include skills that the rider has previously mastered. Modify the routine as new skills are developed. Pre-ride safety routines from basic to more advanced are detailed in the last section of this book, 'Vaulting and Simulation Activities'. The following is an example of a basic pre-ride safety routine, which will take about two minutes to complete, after doing the neck exercises. The helmet and body protector (if worn during riding) should be worn when doing the pre-ride safety routine.

Basic Pre-ride Safety Routine #1		Safe to do unsupervised once mastered.
Height progression: N/A	**Surface progression:** Tumbling mat Grass/turf	**Speed progression:** N/A
Prerequisites: General warm-up and neck-conditioning exercises. Wear the helmet and body protector when doing the pre-ride safety routine.		
STEP 1) From riding position, snap the arms quickly into the brace position, then fall backward and complete rock and roll three times, standing after the third one and finishing in landing position		

Simulate hands holding the reins.	Strong arms with muscle tension.	Maintain a tight tuck with knees slightly apart moving the arms to rock.	Stand without using the hands.	Landing position, with muscle tension in the arms.

STEP 2) Kneel down, move the arms into riding position, snap to the brace position three times. Place the hands on the ground (directly under the shoulders), move into angry cat position and hold three seconds. Raise the knees off the ground to 4-point landing position and complete three push-ups maintaining a rigid body shape. Touch the head gently on the ground with each push-up, then stand.

| Simulate hands holding the reins. | Strong arms with muscle tension. | Rounded back, push through the shoulders, head-in. | Move into 4-point landing position. | Touch the head on each push-up, maintain a rigid body shape. |

STEP 3) Move into riding position and hold two seconds. Fall forward, move the arms quickly into the brace position and continue into a forward roll to landing position. Hold the landing position for two seconds, then stand.

| Simulate hands holding the reins. | Strong arms with muscle tension. | Maintain a tight tuck position with knees slightly apart and back rounded. | Stand without using the hands, with arms in the brace position. | Finish in landing position, with muscle tension in the arms. |

STEP 4) Walk or jog one or two steps forward and then do a small jump with 45-degree turn left to 4-point landing position and continue into a sideways roll to landing position. Then stand. Repeat, except this time do a small jump with 45-degree turn right to 4-point landing position and continue into a sideways roll to landing position. Then stand and turn 180 degrees to face the opposite direction.

Skill learning and training methods

Small jump with 45-degree turn left to 4-point landing position.	Continue into sideways roll, hands turned slightly in, head between the arms.	Maintain tuck position, arms strong and in the brace position.	Jump with 45-degree turn right to 4-point landing position.	Continue into sideways roll, finishing in landing position.

REPEAT the full routine, STEP 1) to STEP 4) facing the opposite direction, excluding the neck exercises.

Food for thought

Performing a pre-ride safety routine takes only a couple of minutes—about the same time as brushing your teeth. If you do not bother to regularly brush your teeth, think of the consequences. Regularly brushing your teeth does not guarantee that you will not have some dental problems. But not brushing them would certainly result in additional visits to the dentist over time.

Fall safety training does not guarantee that you will not be injured in a fall, but learning fall safety skills will certainly reduce the risks.

Warming-up for Fall Safety Training Sessions

Fall safety training sessions should commence with warm-up activities. It is recommended to include activities such as those detailed in the section 'Five Elements for Pre-ride Warm-up' with the fifth element being a pre-ride safety routine. The skills included in a pre-ride safety routine should be learned during fall safety training sessions prior to doing them in a pre-ride safety routine. Warm-up time and warm-up activities should be based on the goals of the training session and the time available for the training. The following is a guideline:

1-hour training session	10 minutes
1.5-hour training session	15 minutes
2-hour training session	20 minutes

As a part of, or following on from, the warm-up, riders should practice body shapes and positions and refine their skills in these basics.

Body Shapes and Basic Positions

A number of 'positions' have been referred to in previous sections of this book. Basic body shapes and positions can easily be practiced by riders of all ages, giving them the foundations for skills development and good fall safety technique. The more these basics are practiced, the better. They can easily be incorporated into warm-up, fitness, or other training activities and will improve the rider's ability to intuitively adopt a good body shape in a fall.

Practicing basic shapes and positions will assist riders to develop and maintain skills such as good feet-first landing technique when dismounting, being able to roll more intuitively when landing off balance, and being able to tuck-and-roll in a high-speed fall.

HELMET AND BODY PROTECTOR (PROTECTIVE CLOTHING)

For comfort and convenience, warm-up, flexibility, and muscle conditioning exercises can be done without wearing protective clothing. It is recommended that riders learn the body shapes, positions, and skills without wearing protective clothing. This will ensure that the skills can be learned with good technique. Once mastered, riders should do some practice of the skills wearing their protective clothing. The body protector should not impede a rider's ability to tuck-and-roll.

IMPORTANT SAFETY NOTE: If the body protector impedes a rider's ability to tuck-and-roll or perform other skills such as a dive roll, then riders should change their body protector to one that is more flexible.

Riders should also wear their protective clothing before progressing tumbling skills to a grass/turf surface. This will provide some additional protection on harder landing surfaces. Performing the skills wearing protective clothing is important for skills transfer—from training to a real fall scenario. The pre-ride safety routine, which takes only a couple of minutes, is recommended to be performed before riding activity on any day, and should be done wearing protective clothing.

Summary of Body Shapes and Positions

Summary of Body Shapes and Positions	Page
Brace position	63
Tuck and open tuck position	64
Landing position	65
Angry cat position	66
4-point landing position	67
Backward candle	68

Skill learning and training methods

Brace Position		Safe to do unsupervised
Height progression: N/A	**Surface progression:** N/A	**Speed progression:** N/A
Prerequisites: Nil		

Key points:

- Head neutral.
- Hands turned in at a 45-degree angle.
- Elbows very slightly bent.
- Biceps and triceps flexed (strong arms).
- Arms between horizontal and vertical.
- Fingers together.

Riders should land with their arms in this position when dismounting from their horse. By practicing this position each time they dismount, riders will develop good landing habits and not need to consciously think about what to do with their arms in a fall.

The brace position can be practiced from a number of different starting positions. For example,

- from standing to the brace position,
- from sitting to the brace position,
- from kneeling to the brace position, and
- from riding position to the brace position.

When applying the brace position to tumbling skills and drills, there will be a natural variation in the angle of the arms from perpendicular to the torso (in a 4-point landing), to almost parallel to the torso (in a dive roll).

More closed arm angle	45-degree arm angle	More open arm angle
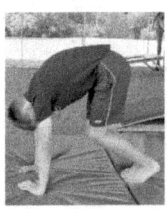		
4-point landing position	Landing position	Dive roll drill

Tuck and Open Tuck Position		Safe to do unsupervised
Height progression: N/A	**Surface progression:** Tumbling mat Grass/turf	**Speed progression:** N/A

Prerequisites: Nil	
Tuck position: 	**Key points:** • Arms in the brace position with muscle tension (strong arms). • Hands turned in at a 45-degree angle. • Knees bent and slightly apart. • Back rounded. • Head in between the arms. • Abdominal and hip muscles flexed (to maintain a rigid body shape).
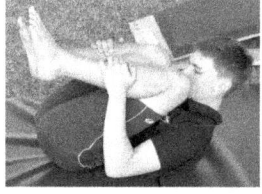	
In gymnastics, trampoline, diving, and other sports that involve somersaulting, the tuck position often includes holding onto the lower leg (shins) in order to somersault very quickly. Holding onto the shins is not recommended for riders when somersaulting. In a fall at speed, a rider will often be forced to roll very quickly after impacting the ground. Having the arms in the brace position will ensure that the rider is better positioned to protect their head and neck when tumbling at speed.	
Open tuck position: 	**Key points:** • Same as tuck position, except the body is more extended, with the knees only slightly bent. • This can be used as a conditioning exercise to develop abdominal and hip flexor muscle strength.

Skill learning and training methods

Landing Position		**Safe to do unsupervised**
Height progression: N/A	**Surface progression:** Tumbling mat Grass/turf	**Speed progression:** N/A

Key points:

- Head neutral (looking forward).
- Arms in the brace position.
  - hands turned in at a 45-degree angle
  - fingers together
  - arms between horizontal and vertical
  - biceps and triceps flexed (strong arms)
- Stomach in (posterior pelvic tilt) so that lower back is straight.
- Knees bent 90-degrees and aligned with the ankles.
- Feet turned out at a 45-degree angle (to avoid ankle sprain).*

The arm muscles, including the biceps and triceps, should be tense at the moment of landing. The instructor or a training partner can reinforce this by applying pressure to the arms with the rider resisting. Include feet-first landing practice in warm-up, fitness, and basic training activities to reduce the risk of ankle sprain and back injury.

* Land in this position when dismounting from your horse—it will ensure that you develop good feet-first landing habits reducing the risk of ankle sprain.

Angry Cat Position		Safe to do unsupervised
Height progression: N/A	**Surface progression:** Tumbling mat Grass/turf	**Speed progression:** N/A
Prerequisites: Nil		

Key points:

- Head in between arms.
- Arms in the brace position.
  - hands turned in at a 45-degree angle
  - fingers together
  - shoulders over the hands
- Lower and upper back rounded, pushing up through the shoulders.

From angry cat position, riders can raise their knees off the ground and move into 4-point landing position.

Happy cat position   Angry cat position   4-point landing position

 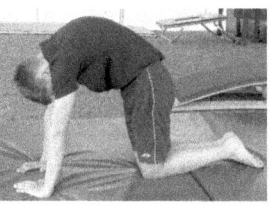 

Hand position:

When doing activities and skills where the hands impact the ground, such as body shapes, forward roll, handstand roll, and dive roll, develop the habit of having the hands turned in slightly at about a 45-degree angle. The fingers also should not be spread too far apart. The correct hand position can be easily developed as a habit with some practice. This will reduce the risk and severity of injury to the fingers, wrists, and possible elbow hyperextension during a high impact landing.

Skill learning and training methods

4-point Landing Position		Safe to do unsupervised
Height progression: N/A	**Surface progression:** Tumbling mat Grass/turf	**Speed progression:** N/A

Prerequisites: Angry cat position.

Key points:

- Head in between the arms.
- Arms in the brace position.
  - Hands turned in at a 45-degree angle
  - Fingers together
  - Shoulders directly above the hands
  - Biceps and triceps flexed (strong arms)
- Back rounded, pushing up through the shoulders.

Include 4-point landing position in warm-up, fitness, and basic training activities. It should also be included as a part of a pre-ride safety routine.

This is the safest way to impact the ground in forward and sideways falls where the rider is falling at a prone or near prone angle, particularly when travelling at speed. When travelling at speed, the rider is likely to be flipped or rotated forward and/or sideways. The 4-point landing position can protect the rider's head and neck from vertical impact force and enable them to continue into a forward or sideways roll sequence without having to change their body shape.

Muscle conditioning: When doing push-ups from the 4-point landing position, maintain a rigid body shape and gently touch the head with each push-up.

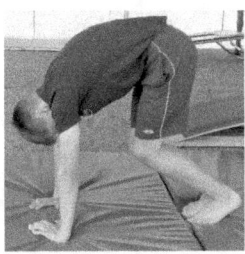 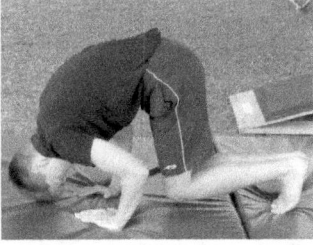 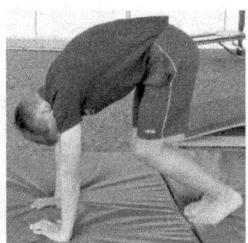

Backward Candle		Safe to do unsupervised
Height progression: N/A	**Surface progression:** Tumbling mat Grass/turf	**Speed progression:** N/A

Prerequisites: The brace position. Rock and roll.

Key points:

- Back rounded, maintain an open tuck position.
- Arms in the brace position.
  - Hands turned in
  - Fingers together
  - Biceps and triceps flexed (strong arms)
- Strong backward arm movement to protect the head and neck.
- Knees slightly bent.

This position may be easier to learn with assistance from an instructor or partner.

Alternatively, the rider can achieve this position temporarily from rock and roll backward or rolling backward down a foam incline.

Basic Rolling and Tumbling Skills

Having the skill to perform rolls in all directions—forward, sideways, and backward—is essential for riders. Most riders should be able to learn a basic forward and sideways roll within a couple of training sessions. It may, however, take longer to learn a backward roll. Even if the backward roll technique is not fully mastered, doing the lead-up activities such as a half roll backward to candle position, and learning how to use the arms to protect the head and neck will provide some protection in a backward fall.

Basic rolling skills are a prerequisite to other more advanced activities. They can also be included in a pre-ride safety routine so that the skills can be retained for a long time.

If riders have not practiced rolling skills (or have not recently practiced rolling skills), it is normal to experience some temporary dizziness and, if a lot of rolling practice is done in one training session, riders may also experience some nausea. Subject to the safety considerations outlined in the Introduction, this is normal and should subside quickly after finishing the training session. It will be less of an issue at subsequent training sessions as riders adapt to the effects of the training.

To minimise the effects of dizziness and/or nausea, the training session should be structured so that rolling activities only form a part of the training session, commensurate with the rider's skill and prior training in these activities. Limit the amount of rolling practice in a single training session and include other activities such as body shapes and positions, flexibility exercises, muscle conditioning, basic jumps, and landing practice. If the training session has variety, it will be more enjoyable for riders.

Once the basic techniques have been mastered, include some practice wearing protective clothing to prepare for tumbling activities on harder surfaces.

Index for Basic Rolling and Tumbling Skills

	Page
Forward roll	70
Sideways shoulder roll	72
Egg roll	73
Backward roll	74
Dive roll drill	75
Handstand roll	76

Forward Roll		Safe to do unsupervised
Height progression: N/A	**Surface progression:** Tumbling mat Grass/turf	**Speed progression:** N/A

Prerequisites: 4-point landing position. Rock and roll.

Key points:

- Commence in 4-point landing position, with the head in between the arms, backside raised and upper back rounded.
- Push-off with the feet so that the head clears the mat and the initial impact is on the shoulders/upper back.
- Maintain tuck position during the roll, with knees slightly apart and the arms in the brace position.
- Stand without pushing off the ground with the hands, so that the arms can reach forward and remain in the brace position (arm muscles tensed).
- Finish in landing position.

Riders may be tempted to grab their shins to assist in the rolling motion and/or push off the ground with their hands when standing up. While this may make standing easier, it is not recommended for riders to use these techniques. Maintaining the arms in the brace position is the safest option when tumbling at speed and in a multiple roll sequence. Developing the habit of having the arms in the brace position during a forward roll is the safest position in a fall—particularly where there is not enough time to consciously think about what to do.

Skill learning and training methods

Forward Roll (continued)

Learning progression: Rock and Roll

Key points:

- Maintain a rigid tuck position.
- Use the arms (as a pendulum) for initiating and maintaining the rocking motion rather than changing body shape.
- Riders who struggle to maintain the tuck position when doing rock and roll should include abdominal curls in their exercise regime to strengthen the middle part of their body.
- After learning how to rock backward and forward a few times, riders should finish by reaching forward and rolling to stand, maintaining the arms in the brace position.

Head exposed to impact with the ground in a fall incident at speed.

 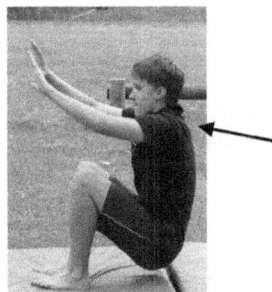

With the arms in brace position the head has protection in a multiple roll scenario.

Sideways Shoulder Roll		Safe to do unsupervised
Height progression: N/A	**Surface progression:** Tumbling mat Grass/turf	**Speed progression:** N/A

Prerequisites: 4-point landing position. Forward roll

Sideways shoulder roll—left shoulder leading (head looking right):

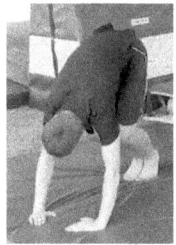   

Sideways shoulder roll—right shoulder leading (head looking left):

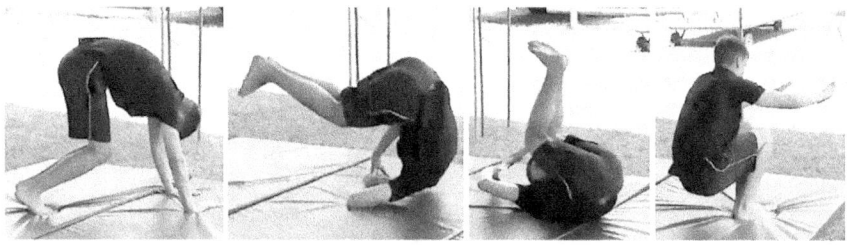

Key points:
- Commence in 4-point landing position.
- Head should be in between the arms and turned slightly (looking in the opposite direction to the roll).
- Push-off with the feet and drop the leading shoulder with the leading elbow in close to the torso. The initial impact should be on the shoulders/upper back.
- Maintain a tuck position (muscles tensed) during the roll, with the knees slightly apart and the arms in the brace position.
- Stand without pushing off the ground with the hands, so the arms can remain in the brace position (arm muscles tensed).
- Finish facing the same direction as the starting position.

Sideways shoulder roll should be practiced on both sides, but riders may find it easier to learn and practice the roll on their preferred side. Once the roll can be performed with basic proficiency on the preferred side, it should be also learned and practiced on the other side.

Skill learning and training methods

Egg Roll		Safe to do unsupervised
Height progression: N/A`	**Surface progression:** Tumbling mat Grass/turf	**Speed progression:** N/A

Prerequisites: Tuck position.

Egg roll down a foam wedge:

Egg roll down a small grass embankment (approximately 30-degree incline):

This skill can be learned and practiced on a foam wedge or on a short grass embankment. If the skill is learned using a foam wedge, it is recommended to progress by also performing the skill down a small grass embankment with protective clothing—to provide a more realistic simulation of rolling in a fall.

Key points:
- Commence in 4-point landing position.
- Maintain the arms in the brace position.
- Maintain the body shape in a tuck position/egg shape.
- The body shape should not change when rolling; the rider should not relax or allow their body position to extend.
- The head should be tucked-in and not impact the mat/ground when rolling.
- The rider should complete at least three rolls, maintaining the egg shape, before coming to rest.
- Practice the skill on both sides.

Backward Roll		Safe to do unsupervised once mastered
Height progression: N/A	**Surface progression:** Landing mat Tumbling mat Grass/turf	**Speed progression:** N/A

Prerequisites: Rock and roll. Half backward roll to candle position.

Key points:

- Learn using a foam incline wedge.
- Do not wear a helmet when first learning this skill as it may place extra pressure on the neck if the arm movement has not been mastered properly.
- Commence in a squat position (or sitting on an incline wedge), with the arms in the brace position.
- Roll backward moving the arms strongly backward to protect the head and neck.
- The body position should remain tucked with muscle tension in the arms.
- Finish in landing position.

Learning progression: Half backward roll to candle position:

Practice the initial movement sequence to master the arm movement without the backward roll when first learning this skill. The backward roll may take longer to learn than forward or sideways roll, so be patient in practicing the half backward roll to candle position using a strong arm movement to protect the head and neck from the initial impact force. Once this learning progression can be performed easily without any significant impact on the head or neck, continue into a backward roll with qualified instructor assistance initially.

Skill learning and training methods

Dive Roll Drill		Safe to do unsupervised once mastered
Height progression: N/A	**Surface progression:** Landing mat Tumbling mat Grass/turf	**Speed progression:** N/A
Prerequisites: Forward roll.		

Place the block against a solid object (such as a tree or wall) to prevent it from moving when the rider pushes off with their feet. The feet should be raised onto a platform of between 60 and 90 cm (2 and 3 ft). The position should be held for a few seconds, then push off with the feet and complete a forward roll smoothly.

A qualified instructor should provide assistance when learning the skill to ensure that the rider's head does not impact the mat.

Key points:
- Start from 4-point landing position with hands close to the block.
- Walk the feet up so the feet are resting on the edge of the block.
- Walk the hands backward towards the block to achieve the correct vertical torso position (as shown).
- The head should be tucked in between the arms and hands turned in at a 45-degree angle.
- The back should be rounded.
- Push off the block with the feet to complete the forward roll.
- The head should not touch the mat when rolling.
- Roll to stand keeping arms in the brace position.

Handstand Roll		Safe to do unsupervised once mastered
Height progression: N/A	**Surface progression:** Landing mat Tumbling mat Grass/turf	**Speed progression:** N/A

Prerequisites: Dive roll drill. Supported handstand roll with assistance.

Key points:
- Commence from stand with the arms in the brace position.
- Step forward into a lunge position (bending the front knee), and place the hands on the ground with the hands turned in at about a 45-degree angle.
- As the hands are placed on the ground, swing the back leg up.
- Join the feet together, keeping the back straight and head between the arms.
- As the momentum carries the rider to a vertical position, tuck the head in (chin to chest) and continue into a forward roll.
- The initial impact with the ground should be on the shoulders/upper back and not on the head, and the roll should be smooth.
- Roll to stand in landing position.

Learning progression #1: Supported handstand—front to landing mat, then roll.

Handstand roll learning progression #1 (continued)

Key points:

- Place a landing mat against a wall or other secure object (at a slight angle so the mat does not fall down when the rider pushes off the mat).
- Place the hands on the ground near the mat and then 'walk the feet up'.
- Shuffle the hands in so they are close to or touching the mat.
- Head should be in between the arms and the back should be straight.
- Hands turned in slightly.
- Hold the position for up to twenty seconds to learn the correct body shape and to build up strength in the arms and shoulders. Riders who are not as strong in their arms may need to hold the position for a shorter time and build the time up over a few practice sessions.
- After holding the handstand position, gently push off the mat with the feet and continue into a forward roll.
- As the rider rolls forward, the head should be tucked in so that the initial impact is on the shoulders/upper back.
- This activity should be performed initially with an instructor assisting to ensure that the rider rolls smoothly after pushing off the mat.
- Use a mat for the roll when learning this progression.

Learning progression #2: Kick to handstand and roll with assistance.

When practicing the above supported handstand drills, it is beneficial to remain in the handstand position briefly in order to learn the correct body shape and to build up muscle strength in the arms. When doing an unsupported handstand roll, there is no need to hold the handstand position—simply continue into a forward roll. Balancing in a handstand position requires a lot of practice and does not provide any additional benefit to riders in fall safety skills. Once the rider can perform a handstand roll consistently on a landing mat, progress to performing the skill on a tumbling mat and then to grass/turf wearing protective clothing.

Basic Aerial Skills

This section covers basic aerial skills development. Aerial skills are those which require 'flight time' or time travelling through the air. The flight time may be very short—coming down from a low height—or longer—coming down from a greater height.

Some aerial skills are basic and can be practiced unsupervised, such as a simple straight jump to a feet-first landing position. These basic aerial skills can be learned and practiced during the initial training sessions when the rider is learning other skills including body shapes and basic rolling techniques.

Once basic aerial and landing skills have been mastered, they can be performed in various combinations. After a few training sessions of practicing a variety of landing and rolling combinations, most riders will start to perform the movement sequences more intuitively.

More advanced aerial and tumbling skills such as jumps at speed, dive roll, forward somersault, or jumps using obstacles can be learned after the basic aerial skills have been mastered. When doing basic aerial skills, include some practice wearing protective clothing as a preparation for landing on harder surfaces and as a preparation for the more advanced activities that follow.

Index for Basic Aerial Skills	**Page**
Basic Jumps	79
• Straight jump	
• Star jump	
• Tuck jump	
• Jump half turn	
Jump, Land and Roll	83
• Straight jump + forward roll	
• Star jump + forward roll	
• Tuck Jump + forward roll	
• Jump half turn + backward roll	
• Jump to 4-point landing + sideways roll	

Basic Jumps		Safe to do unsupervised
Height progression: Low Moderate High	**Surface progression:** Tumbling mat Grass/turf	**Speed progression:** N/A

Prerequisites: Landing position.

Basic jumps can be practiced by all riders with minimal equipment.

Straight jump from ground level:

Key points:

- Swing the arms up and into the brace position on take-off.
- Head neutral (not extended backward or flexed forward).
- Hold the landing position for one to two seconds to check landing technique.
- Progress from ground level to a 30 cm (1 ft) take-off height and then to a 60 cm (2 ft) take-off height.
- Progress from tumbling mats to landing on grass/turf when ready.

Straight jump—30 cm (1 ft) take-off height:

Straight jump—60 cm (2 ft) take-off height:

Basic Jumps (continued)	Safe to do unsupervised

Star jump from ground level:

After practicing the straight jump to the correct landing position, riders should be able to quickly learn this variation in body position when in the air. The purpose of this exercise is—in a situation where a rider may be thrown or falling from their horse in a 'spread eagle position' or with arms and legs apart—to develop the skill to return quickly to a closed body position when impacting the ground.

Key points:

- Swing the arms upward and jump up with two-feet take-off.
- Move the arms and legs apart into the star position and then quickly bring the feet together and the arms back into the brace position before landing.
- Bend the knees when landing and finish in landing position.

Star jump—30 cm (1 ft) take-off height:	Star jump—60 cm (2 ft) take-off height:

Basic Jumps (continued)	Safe to do unsupervised

Tuck jump from ground level:

Key points:

- Swing the arms upward to the brace position when jumping, using the same take-off as straight jump.
- Quickly bring the knees up into the tuck position with the arms remaining in the brace position.
- Move from tuck position to open tuck position when landing. The arm position should not change.

Tuck jump—30 cm (1 ft) take-off height:	Tuck jump—60 cm (2 ft) take-off height:

Basic Jumps (continued)	Safe to do unsupervised

Jump half turn from ground level:

Key points:
- Swing the arms upward when jumping and commence the turn at the peak of the jump.
- The arms should be in the brace position on landing.
- Practice the half turn in both directions (turning to the left and to the right).

Jump half turn—30 cm (1 ft) take-off height:	Jump half turn—60 cm (2 ft) take-off height:

Turn direction = Right	Turn direction = Left

Skill learning and training methods

Jump, Land, and Roll		Safe to do unsupervised once mastered
Height progression: Low Moderate High	**Surface progression:** Tumbling mat Grass/turf	**Speed progression:** N/A

Prerequisites: Basic jumps from 60 cm (2 ft) height. Basic rolling skills.

After learning basic aerial skills and rolling techniques, riders can progress by performing these skills in various combinations. When doing a combination activity for the first time, do the activity at ground level on tumbling mats before progressing in height or to a grass/turf landing surface. The following is an example of height and surface progression:

- Ground level on tumbling mats.
- 30 cm (1 ft) take-off height, landing on tumbling mats.
- 60 cm (2 ft) take-off height, landing on tumbling mats.
- Ground level on grass, wearing protective gear.
- 30 cm (1 ft) take-off height, landing on grass, wearing protective gear.
- 60 cm (2 ft) take-off height, landing on grass, wearing protective gear.

EXAMPLES OF COMBINATION ACTIVITIES:

Straight jump + forward roll: height 60 cm (2 ft) to tumbling mats:

Key points:

- Arms in the brace position when airborne.
- Land at a slight forward angle to facilitate rolling.
- Bend the knees approximately 90-degrees on landing.
- Tuck the head in during the forward roll so impact is on the shoulders not on the head.
- Knees slightly apart during the forward roll.
- Roll smoothly and maintain the arms in the brace position when standing.

Jump, Land, and Roll (continued)	Safe to do unsupervised once mastered

Star jump, land and forward roll: height 30 cm (1 ft) to tumbling mats:

Tuck jump, land and forward roll: height 60 cm (2 ft) to tumbling mats:

Jump half turn land and backward roll: height 60 cm (2 ft) to tumbling mats:

REMEMBER: Increase the knee bend when landing from greater heights.

Jump, Land, and Roll (continued)	Safe to do unsupervised once mastered

Jump 45-degree turn left to 4-point landing and sideways roll: tumbling mats:

Key points:

- The head should be tucked in between the arms and under the non-leading arm/shoulder.
- Ensure the correct 4-point landing position is achieved when commencing the sideways roll.
- Practice this skill on both sides, initially on the preferred side, and then jump with a 45-degree turn to the other side.
- Maintain tuck position with arms in the brace position during the roll.
- Because the arms and the legs are breaking the fall together in the 4-point landing position, progress this activity to greater heights and harder landing surfaces slower than other jumps activities—the arms have approximately 50 per cent of the relative strength of the legs.
- Add some variation by commencing the movement from riding position and simulate letting go of the reins.

Jump 45-degree turn right to 4-point landing and sideways roll: 60 cm (2 ft):

Height, Landing Surface, and Speed Progression

Height Progression

Once confident in jumping and landing from ground level and at moderate height, riders should aim to develop the height of their aerial skills to simulate coming down from horse height. With an average horse height being approximately 160 cm (5.2 ft) or 16 hands, the height of a rider's centre of gravity in riding position will be about 40 cm (16 in) above this point or 2 m (6.6 ft) above the ground (160 + 40 cm).

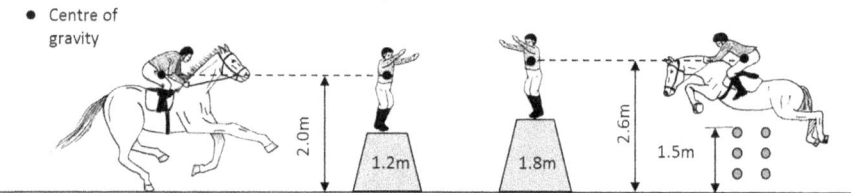

Therefore, learning aerial skills by jumping from a platform of 120 cm (4 ft)—where the centre of gravity is at a height of approximately 2 m (6.6 ft)—will simulate the vertical fall height for most horse riding activities. Sometimes, riders will be coming down from a lower height—for example, pony riders—and sometimes from a greater height—for example, in a jumps activity or where a rider is bucked into the air. Riders who are involved in a jumps activity such as a hurdle or steeplechase race, or a showjumping or cross-country event, should progress aerial skills to jumping from a platform of between 150 and 180 cm (5 and 6 ft).

When practicing aerial skills from greater heights, softer landing surfaces such as a crashmat should be used initially. The landing surface can be gradually progressed to firmer surfaces and finally to a tumbling mat or grass/turf. Wear protective clothing when practicing the skills on harder landing surfaces. A mini-tramp can also be used for jumping activities, using a short 5 m (16 ft) approach jog. When using a mini-tramp, estimate the height by observing the difference between the rider's centre of gravity at the peak of the trajectory and the landing surface. The centre of gravity is a point in the middle of the body slightly below the belly button.

The following is an example of how aerial skills can be gradually progressed to higher levels and to harder landing surfaces. Note that this is a guideline only: the progression should be based on the rider being proficient at one level before progressing to the next level.

Skill learning and training methods

Platform height	Surface	Progression
30 cm (1 ft)	Grass/turf	
60 cm (2 ft)	Tumbling mat	Increased height, softer surface
90 cm (3 ft)	Landing mat	Increased height, softer surface
120 cm (4 ft)	Crashmat	Increased height, softer surface
120 cm (4 ft)	Landing mat	Same height, harder surface
120 cm (4 ft)	Tumbling mat	Same height, harder surface
120 cm (4 ft)	Grass/turf	Same height, harder surface

When landing on harder surfaces, riders should bend their knees more so the impact forces are absorbed over a greater time (but not landing in a full squat position, as this may cause knee injury).

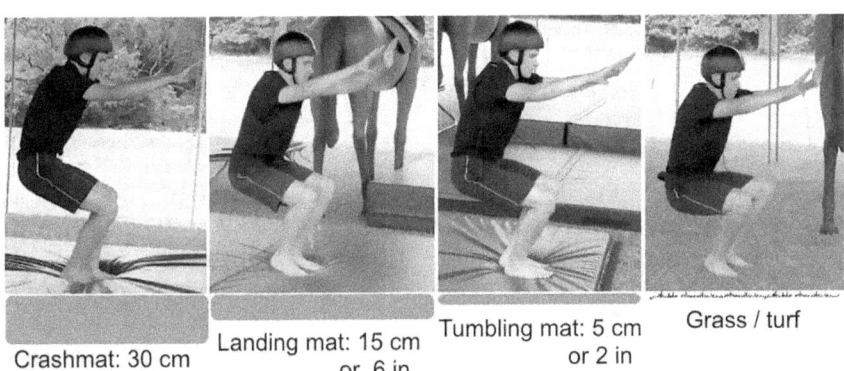

Crashmat: 30 cm or 12 in   Landing mat: 15 cm or 6 in   Tumbling mat: 5 cm or 2 in   Grass / turf

Speed Progression

It is also important for riders to progress from low-speed to higher-speed scenarios once they master the basics of coming down and rolling from a height. Increasing the speed when performing aerial skills can be achieved by adding an approach run and using cones to mark the run distance.

Approach run (distance)	Speed	Horse gait
Jogging 5 to 10 m (16 to 33 ft)	up to 10 km/h (6 mph)	Walking
Running: 10 to 20 m (16 to 66 ft)	up to 20 km/h (12 mph)	Trot/slow canter
Sprint: 20 to 30 m (33 to 99 ft)	up to 30 km/h (18 mph)	Slow gallop

When using a faster approach run of 20 to 30 km/h (12 to 18 mph)—a fast run—it is not recommended to use a mini-tramp for take-off. The mini-tramp is better for take-off at slower speeds where the goal is to achieve greater height rather than horizontal speed. Jumps from higher speed can be better performed using an airboard or spring-board.

Mini-trampoline	Air-board / spring-board

From a fast run, riders can use a single foot take-off from the air-board or spring-board. A spring-board has similar rebound properties to an air-board, except that it uses coil springs instead of airbags. An air-board or spring-board will better preserve the horizontal speed at the point of take-off. Speeds of between 20 to 30 km/h (12 to 18 mph) may be achieved from a fast approach run. When jumping and landing feet-first from a fast run, riders should not attempt to stop their momentum but should continue into a roll. Riders should master combination activities of landing followed by a roll at low and moderate speeds before progressing to higher speeds.

HIGHER SPEEDS

Riding activities such as racing involve higher speeds—approximately 60 km/h (40 mph). Riders who have mastered fall safety skills from heights of 120 to 180 cm (4 to 6 ft) and speeds of up to 30 km/h (18 mph) will have considerably more protection in a high-speed fall than riders who are untrained. The techniques for landing at higher speeds are not significantly different from those required for landing at 20 to 30 km/h (12 to 18 mph). The difference is that increased fitness and strength is required to cope with the increased forces of angular momentum in higher speed falls, rather than a difference in tumbling technique being required.

Fall time to the ground and the available time for response action is a function of the height of the fall and not horizontal speed. It is very important for riders who engage in high-speed horse riding activities to be trained in fall safety skills so they can mitigate the significant forces of angular momentum by using a tuck-and-roll technique at the point of impact with the ground. It is also important that riders let go of the reins as soon as they realise they are falling, otherwise the rider will lose control of their body shape when the reins become taut and risk significant blunt force impact to the head and neck.

In high-speed falls at the point of impact with the ground, the rider should have their arms in the brace position and be in (or moving into) a tuck position. Once the tuck position is achieved with the arms in the brace position, the rider should use all their available strength to hold themselves in this position, allowing their horizontal momentum to continue for as long as possible. Further detail of this standard fall safety technique is covered in the Theory and Science section—Fall Safety Technique Analysis.

Skill learning and training methods

Direction of travel ⟶

4-point landing   forward roll   sideways roll   sideways roll   backward roll

In a high-speed fall, the rider may impact the ground in a number of different directions: forward, sideways, backward, feet-first, upside down, prone (4-point landing). As shown above, once the rider begins to roll, the body shape is essentially the same irrespective of the direction of travel. If the rider is aware that they are rolling backward, the main difference in this scenario is that the arms should move backward strongly to reduce the impact force on the head and neck. The body position should remain tucked, with muscle tension.

In a higher speed fall, once a rider is in a roll sequence they should not attempt to stop their momentum or change their direction of travel—but stay tucked with the arms in the brace position to protect their head and neck and continue to roll in any direction.

Index for Height, Landing Surface, and Speed Progression Page

Height and Surface Progression   90

- Jump, land + forward or sideways roll
- Jump to 4-point landing + sideways roll
- Jump half turn + backward roll

Speed Progression   94

- Jump, land + forward roll
- Jump, land + sideways roll
- Multiple incline roll

Height and Surface Progression

Height progression: Moderate High Advanced	Surface progression: Crashmat Landing mat Tumbling mat Grass/turf	Speed progression: N/A

Prerequisites: Jump, land and roll from 60 cm (2 ft).

After practicing combination activities of jump, land and roll from 60 cm (2 ft), riders can progress by performing these skills from a greater jump height. When progressing to a greater height, riders should initially perform the skills landing on a softer surface. Once the skills are performed consistently well, they can be progressed to harder landing surfaces. Height progression can be done in 30 cm (1 ft) increments until the target height is reached. Only progress to a higher level or to a harder landing surface if the skill has been mastered at the previous level or surface.

- Jump, land + forward roll
- Jump to 4-point landing + sideways roll (practice on both sides)
- Jump half turn, land + backward roll

EXAMPLES OF JUMP, LAND, AND ROLL FROM HEIGHT:

Straight jump + forward roll: 120 cm (4 ft) platform to tumbling mats

Key points:

- Land feet-first at a slight forward angle to facilitate rolling.
- Remember to have the feet turned out slightly to avoid ankle sprain.
- Tuck the head in during the forward roll so impact is on the shoulders not on the head.
- Have your knees slightly apart during the forward roll.
- Roll smoothly and maintain the arms in the brace position when standing.
- Vary the activity by starting in riding position.

Height and Surface Progression (continued)

Star jump, land, and forward roll: 120 cm (4 ft) platform to grass:

Jump, 4-point landing, and sideways roll: 90 cm (3 ft) platform to landing mat:

Key points:

- When doing a sideways roll, tuck the head in between the arms.
- Practice 4-point landing and sideways roll on both sides. This should be mastered at ground level before progressing in height.
- Wear protective clothing when landing on harder surfaces.

Height and Surface Progression (continued)

AERIAL SKILLS USING A MINI-TRAMP

Once riders have learned the basic aerial skills jumping from a platform, these skills can also be practiced using an approach run and a mini-tramp with a padded frame. Riders who may not have used a mini-tramp, can familiarise themselves with the take-off surface by stepping from a 60 cm (2 ft) platform, bouncing from the mini-tramp with a two-feet take-off, and landing on a crashmat. Once the rider is familiar with the mini-tramp take-off surface, the platform can be removed and riders can use a short 5 m (16 ft) approach jog. The angle of the mini-tramp can be adjusted based on the speed of approach.

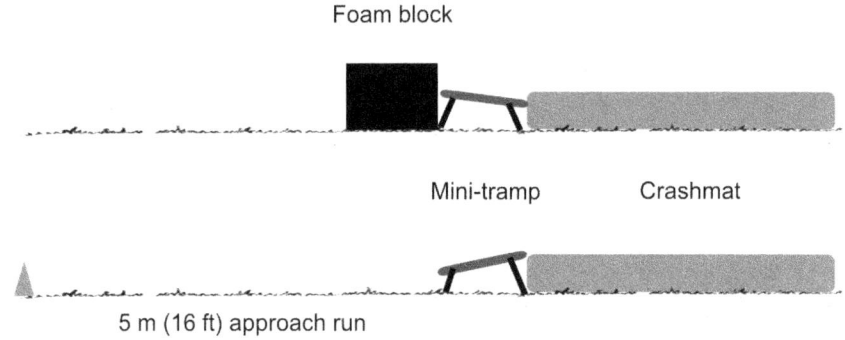

Key points:

- Practice all of the basic jumps and aerial activities from a short 5 m (16 ft) approach run while becoming familiar with the mini-tramp.
- As the speed of the approach run is increased, it is recommended that aerial skills be done in combination with a roll (forward, backward, and sideways depending on the landing direction) so the rider can practice continuing their momentum after they land.
- Because the arms and legs are breaking the fall together in the 4-point landing position, progress this activity to greater heights and harder landing surfaces more slowly than other aerial skills—the arms have approximately 50 per cent of the relative strength of the legs.

Skill learning and training methods

Height and Surface Progression (continued)

EXAMPLES OF BASIC AERIAL SKILLS USING A MINI-TRAMP:

Straight jump   Star jump   Tuck jump   Jump half turn

PROGRESSION:
Once aerial skills have been mastered using a crashmat, they can be progressed to harder landing surfaces—landing mat, tumbling mat, and to grass/turf.

Straight jump, land and forward roll: mini-tramp to a grass surface:

Remember to wear protective clothing when practicing on harder surfaces.

Speed Progression		
Height progression: Low Moderate High	**Surface progression:** Crashmat Landing mat Tumbling mat Grass/turf	**Speed progression:** Low Moderate High

Prerequisites: Jump, land and roll from 120 cm (4 ft) platform to tumbling mat or grass/turf. Basic aerial skills using a mini-tramp and an air-board.

Once the rider has mastered the basic aerial skills in combination with rolling techniques, increase the approach run speed. On progressing to a fast run when doing aerial skills—straight jump, star jump, tuck jump, and jump half turn—it is recommended to use a single foot take-off from an air-board or a spring-board rather than the traditional two-feet take-off. An air-board or a spring-board has a faster rebound action than a mini-tramp and a single-foot take-off will enable the rider to maintain their horizontal momentum and land feet-first before rolling.

20 m (66 ft) fast approach run, using a single foot take-off from an air-board:

Skill learning and training methods

Speed Progression (continued)

Tuck jump, land and forward roll on grass/turf:

Jump, land and sideways roll on grass/turf:

Key points:

- Maintain tuck position with arms in the brace position during the roll sequence.
- Do not try to stop horizontal momentum after the initial landing.
- As speed increases the rider should roll multiple times before coming to rest.
- Do this activity at the end of the training session as it may result in some dizziness.
- Only do a small number of attempts (two or three) in a training session.

Speed Progression (continued)

MULTIPLE INCLINE ROLL

When landing at speed, the rider will be flipped or rotated on landing and at very high-speeds this will include being rolled many times. It is very important that riders do what they can to maintain their momentum as this will dissipate the forces over time and reduce blunt force trauma. Once riders have learned rolling techniques—forward, backward, and sideways—and progressed to higher speeds, it is recommended to do some practice in multiple rolling skills. When practicing on a flat surface, riders will come to rest quite quickly. An incline will assist in maintaining the rider's momentum to better simulate rolling in a higher speed fall. Multiple incline rolls should be progressed gradually from a shorter and smaller incline (initially with tumbling mats). Wear protective clothing when practicing on grass/turf.

Multiple incline roll (approx. 30-degrees) on 10 m (33 ft) of tumbling mats:

Key points:
- Maintain the tuck position and the arms in the brace position.
- There should be minimal head impact on the ground—the arms in the brace position should mitigate the head impact.
- The roll direction may change from forward to sideways. This is normal and riders should not try to resist any change in the direction of travel. The body shape is essentially the same irrespective of the roll direction.
- The rider should not try to stop their momentum but stay tucked until coming to rest.
- Do this activity at the end of a training session and limit the number of attempts to two or three, as riders may experience some nausea or dizziness after doing this activity.

Skill learning and training methods

Speed Progression (continued)

4-point landing and egg roll down a grass incline:

Key points:

- Maintain tuck position and the arms in the brace position.
- There should be minimal head impact on the ground—the arms in the brace position should mitigate any head impact.
- Perform this activity with protective clothing when practicing on a grass surface without tumbling mats.
- Practice the skill on both sides.
- The roll direction may change from sideways to another direction. Riders should not try to resist any change in their direction of rolling. The body shape is essentially the same irrespective of the roll direction.
- The rider should not try to stop their momentum but stay tucked (with muscle tension) until coming to rest, then count to three before standing.
- Do this activity at the end of a training session as riders may experience some nausea or dizziness after doing this activity.

Dive Roll Drills and Skills

The dive roll is a basic gymnastics skill. However, it requires special attention in terms of teaching progression to ensure that it can be safely learned and practiced by riders. Once the basics are mastered consistently and the general safety considerations in the Introduction section are adhered to, most riders should be able to perform a basic dive roll routinely. Once mastered, include this skill in a pre-ride safety routine, after doing general warm-up activities.

The skill of performing a dive roll is important for riders—it is the best way of mitigating serious injury in a head-first fall. Riders should be competent in the prerequisites and progress through the lead-up activities under the supervision of a qualified instructor when learning a dive roll.

This section details basic as well as more advanced dive roll activities including height and speed progression. If the more advanced activities are not achieved by riders, learning a basic dive roll at low height and low speed on a soft landing surface will afford better protection in a head-first fall than being untrained. Riders should not feel compelled to progress beyond their level of capability, skill, or fitness and should progress under the supervision of a qualified instructor.

Dive Roll Body Shape

When performing a dive roll, gymnasts aim to achieve a stretched/layout (completely open) body position during the 'flight phase' for aesthetic reasons. When falling at speed, riders will be forced to roll, sometimes very quickly, following the point of initial impact with the ground. For this reason, riders should not try to achieve a full-body stretch during a dive roll but remain in an open tuck or more closed body shape. This variation in body shape will enable the rider to tuck-and-roll more quickly at the point of initial impact with the ground if landing at speed.

Gymnastics technique of layout position is not recommended for horse riders

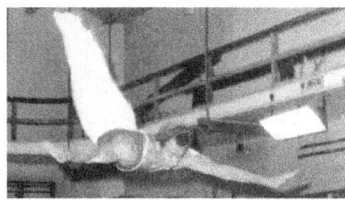

Barry Cheales - former Olympic gymnast and coach

Additional dive roll activities are also included in the section 'Vaulting Skills and Simulation Activities.'

Skill learning and training methods

Index for Dive Roll Drills and Skills   **Page**

Standing Dive Roll   100
- Dive roll drill
- Standing dive roll from low height

Dive Roll from an Approach Run   102
- Low speed, low height
- 5 m (16 ft) approach run

Dive Roll at Height   104
- 90 cm (3 ft) take-off height
- 120 cm (4 ft) take-off height
- Dive roll using a mini-tramp

Dive Roll at Speed   106
- Dive roll using an air-board
- Dive roll + roll, fast approach run

Standing Dive Roll		Safe to do unsupervised once mastered
Height progression: Low Moderate	**Surface progression:** Crashmat Landing mat Tumbling mat Grass/turf	**Speed progression:** N/A

Prerequisites: Forward roll. Straight jump, land and forward roll. Dive roll drill.

Standing dive roll to landing mat—after completion of learning progression:

Key points:
- Commence from landing position.
- Lean forward, maintaining the arms in the brace position.
- Push off with the feet just prior to the hands reaching the ground. When learning this skill, the 'flight time' should be minimal.
- Continue into a forward roll as the hands impact the ground.
- Wrists should be turned in at a 45-degree angle.
- There should be no head impact on the ground.
- Roll to stand without pushing off the ground with the hands, so that the arms can reach forward and remain in the brace position.
- Practice on a softer landing surface until the roll is executed smoothly.
- The qualified instructor should spot (provide assistance) as required.

Learning Progression #1: Dive roll drill on landing mat—feet raised:

Feet should be on a platform of between 60 and 90 cm (2 and 3 ft). Hold the position for a few seconds before completing the roll. Head should be in-between the arms and not touch the ground when rolling. The hands turned in at a 45-degree angle and the back should be round.

Standing Dive Roll (continued)

Learning Progression #2: Standing dive roll from low height—assisted.

Learning Progression #3: Standing dive roll from low height—unassisted.

Once the above progressions have been mastered, the rider should be able to perform a standing dive roll from a 30 cm (1 ft) platform to a crashmat, and then progress to harder landing surfaces wearing protective clothing.

Standing dive roll from 30 cm (1 ft) to landing mat:

Standing dive roll to grass surface wearing protective clothing:

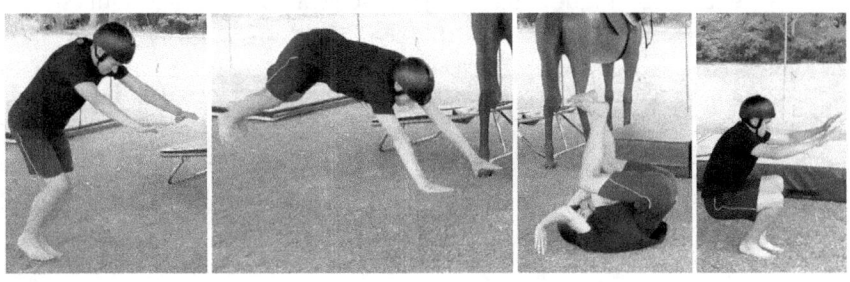

Dive Roll from an Approach Run	Safe to do unsupervised once mastered

Height progression: Low Moderate	**Surface progression:** Crashmat Landing mat Tumbling mat Grass/turf	**Speed progression:** Low Moderate High

Prerequisites: Standing dive roll—unassisted.

Dive roll from a 5 m (16 ft) approach jog:

Equipment set-up:

```
——— 5 m (16 ft) approach ———→
         ——— 3 m (10 ft) approach ——→
▲        ▲
         Tumbling mats              Landing mat
```

Key points:

- Initially perform this skill at low speed and low height—from a short 3 m (10 ft) approach jog—with two-feet take-off and dive roll onto a landing mat.
- Use the same technique as standing dive roll with only a small flight time.
- The qualified instructor should provide some spotting assistance as required.
- Gradually increase to a 5 m (10 ft) approach jog and increase the flight time.

Skill learning and training methods

Dive Roll from an Approach Run (continued)

SURFACE PROGRESSION

Dive roll from 5 m (10 ft) approach run on tumbling mats:

Dive roll from 5 m (10 ft) approach run on grass/turf:

  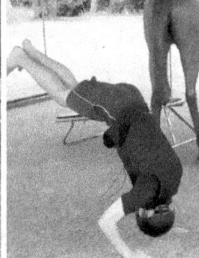 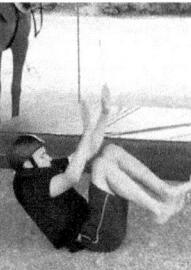

Key points:

Once the dive roll can be performed consistently with a smooth rolling technique on tumbling mats, riders can then progress to a grass/turf landing surface wearing protective clothing.

Dive Roll at Height

Height progression: Moderate High Advanced	Surface progression: Crashmat Landing mat	Speed progression: Standing Low Moderate

Prerequisites: Standing dive roll from a 60 cm (2 ft) platform to crashmat. Dive roll from a 5 m (10 ft) approach run—unassisted. Basic aerial skills.

Standing dive roll to crashmat—height progression 90 then 120 cm (3 then 4 ft)

Foam vaulting box

120 cm (4 ft) platform

90 cm (3 ft) platform

Crashmat

Key points:

- Perform initially with qualified instructor assistance through the movement sequence.
- Commence from landing position or riding position.
- Lean forward maintaining the arms in the brace position.
- The hands should be turned in at a 45-degree angle, and head in between the arms at point of impact with the mat.
- There should be no head impact on the mat. Impact should be on the shoulders/upper back.
- It is not recommended to perform a standing dive roll from heights such as 120 cm (4 ft) to harder landing surfaces—use a crashmat or alternatively a landing mat on top of the crashmat for a firmer surface.

Dive roll using a mini-tramp with a 5 m (16 ft) approach run:

Dive Roll at Height (continued)

Performing a dive roll at height from an approach run is a prerequisite skill for performing a dive roll over any obstacle. The skill should be performed consistently well at the required height before introducing an obstacle such as a vaulting box and simulation activities such as a jumps obstacle or replica horse.

Key points:

- When first attempting this skill, perform with qualified instructor assistance.
- With gradual increase in run-up speed, an improvement in height can be achieved.

Dive roll from mini-tramp: 1.6 m (5.2 ft) height above crashmat surface:

Horse height

1.6 m (5.2 ft)

REMINDER: Hand position when doing dive roll activities.

Dive Roll at Speed		
Height progression: Low Moderate High	**Surface progression:** Crashmat Landing mat Tumbling mat Grass/turf	**Speed progression:** Low Moderate High

Prerequisites: Standing dive roll from 60 cm platform. Dive roll from a 5 m (16 ft) approach run—unassisted. Basic aerial skills using an air-board.

Dive roll using an air-board or spring-board:

Basic aerial skills such as straight jump, star jump, tuck jump and jump half turn can be performed using an air-board as well as a mini-tramp. The take-off from an air-board will be quicker. Riders should practice basic aerial skills using an air-board to become familiar with jumping from an air-board, before progressing to dive roll using an air-board.

Key points:

- Perform initially with qualified instructor assistance through the movement sequence and a short approach run.
- Once the dive roll can be performed consistently well from an air-board, gradually increase the distance and speed of the approach run.
- As the run speed and angular momentum increase, riders should continue into an additional forward or sideways roll following on from the dive roll.

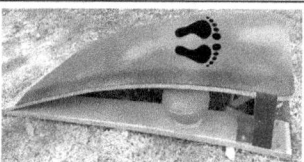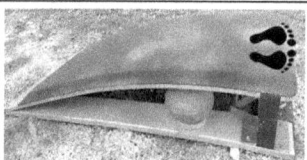

Dive Roll at Speed (continued)

Dive roll from a fast approach run using air-board: multiple roll sequence:

Key points:

- The dive roll should be performed consistently well at low and moderate speed before performing it from a fast approach run.
- Progression should be supervised by a qualified instructor.
- Gradually increase the run distance and speed over multiple training sessions.
- Gradually progress from softer to harder landing surfaces.
- When progressing to higher take-off speeds—after completing the dive roll—remain tucked and continue into additional roll(s) rather than trying to stop the momentum.
- As horizontal speed increases, the rider should tuck quickly at the point of impact with the ground. This will enable the rider to continue into a multiple roll sequence at speed.

REMINDER:

Before practicing on grass/turf, the ground should be inspected to ensure that there are no hazards such as rock, metal, holes, glass, protrusions, tree roots, uneven surfaces or underlying concrete, etc. The grass/turf surface should have some give.

Forward Somersault

Forward somersault is a more advanced skill for riders and can be learned once the basics such as rolling, aerial skills, and dive roll have been mastered. It requires a reasonable level of physical conditioning and should be learned under the supervision of a qualified instructor.

Somersaulting skills will benefit riders by:

- improving kinaesthetic or 'spatial' awareness (of body position in the air);
- increasing the likelihood of landing feet-first if the rider is bucked into a somersault; and
- reducing the risk of the rider trying to see where the ground is when impossible to do so (such as when a rider is rotating at speed).

Wrong response actions with loss of visual orientation include looking up to try to see where the ground is, allowing the body to relax into an open body position, and not having the arms in the brace position with muscle tension to protect the head and neck.

The forward somersault technique for riders is a variation on the standard gymnastic technique. Standard gymnastic technique often includes grasping the shins to pull the body into a tight tuck position to somersault quickly. This enables a gymnast to perform somersaults and multiple somersaults in short timeframes. Riders should perform a somersault in an open tuck position with the arms in the brace position. The direction of impact with the ground may not be known and this is a safer position for riders.

Use a crashmat when initially learning and practicing forward somersault activities. Note that a crashmat provides some additional protection against injury when learning new skills. It cannot prevent all landing injuries and is not a substitute for qualified instruction and proper skills progression.

Index for Forward Somersault	**Page**
Dive roll to raised landing surface	110
Forward somersault landing drill	111
¾ forward somersault on raised landing surface	111
Forward somersault	112
Using a safety belt	113
Forward somersault from approach run	114

Skill learning and training methods

Forward Somersault

Height progression:	Surface progression:	Speed progression:
Low Moderate	Crashmat Landing mat	Low Moderate High

Prerequisites: Dive roll from an approach run—unassisted. Aerial skills using a mini-tramp and an air-board.

Forward somersault from a 5 m (16 ft) approach jog using mini-tramp:

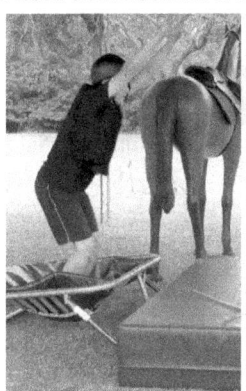 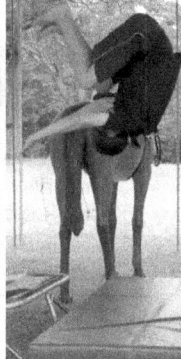  

Key points:
- Master all of the learning progression activities before attempting the forward somersault unassisted.
- Learn the forward somersault on a crashmat at low horizontal speed before progressing to a harder surface and a faster approach run.
- Use a two-feet take-off from a mini-tramp or an air-board.
- The arms should be up and head looking forward at the point of take-off.
- After take-off, move into a tuck position, maintaining the arms in the brace position during the forward somersault.
- Just prior to landing move into an open tuck position and try to spot the ground by looking forward (not down towards the feet)
- Finish in landing position with the knees bent approximately 90-degrees.
- If falling forward when landing, continue into a forward or sideways roll.
- Do not try to stop the momentum.

NOTE: Riders should not grab their shins when doing a somersault.

  Head exposed

Forward Somersault (continued)

The activities for learning the forward somersault can be done using a mini-tramp (in a reverse position) and jumping from a 60 cm (2 ft) raised surface. This will enable the rider to learn the lead-up activities with a consistent take-off position and also allow for a greater number of repetitions before being physically worn out from repeated approach runs. For all learning progression activities, the qualified instructor should provide physical assistance (spotting) as required.

EQUIPMENT SET-UP: FORWARD SOMERSAULT LEARNING PROGRESSION

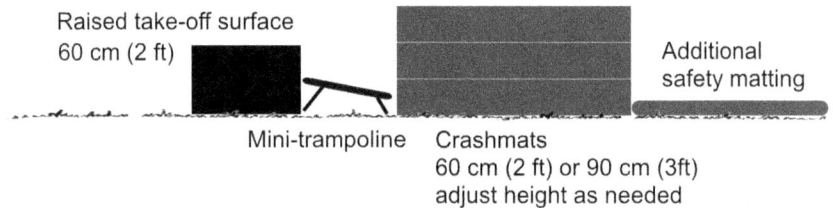

Raised take-off surface 60 cm (2 ft)
Additional safety matting
Mini-trampoline
Crashmats 60 cm (2 ft) or 90 cm (3ft) adjust height as needed

Progression #1: Dive roll to a raised landing surface:

Key points:

- Practice a basic jumping activity, such as a straight jump to a 60 cm (2 ft) landing surface with the mini-tramp in reverse position to become familiar with the equipment set-up.
- Take-off in a vertical position (with only a slight forward lean).
- Achieve some 'flight time' before placing the hands on the mat.
- The head should not impact the mat.
- Continue into the roll maintaining a tuck position with muscle tension.
- As confidence and skill level improves, increase the 'flight time' before the hands touch the mat.

Skill learning and training methods

Forward Somersault (continued)

Progression #2: Forward somersault landing drill

This activity can be practiced at the same time as Progression #1. After doing the dive roll to a raised landing surface, the rider can simply do the forward somersault landing drill when coming down from the crashmat to a landing mat.

Key points:
- Commence from 4-point landing position on the raised surface.
- Push off with the feet to do the forward roll, maintaining a tuck position.
- Keep the arms in the brace position when rolling from the edge of the crashmat.
- Move into an open tuck position and try to spot the ground when landing by looking forward (not down towards the feet).

Progression #3: ¾ forward somersault to raised surface 90 to120 cm (3 to 4 ft):

Key points:
- Once greater flight time is achieved in Progression #1, simply go into a tight tuck position without placing hands on the mat and complete a ¾ somersault, landing seat first on the raised landing surface.
- Keep the arms in the brace position to protect from accidental head impact.

Forward Somersault (continued)

Progression #4: Forward somersault to crashmat using a safety belt:

Once the ¾ forward somersault to a raised landing surface and the forward somersault landing drill have been mastered, the two movement sequences can be combined. Remove the raised landing surface and perform the jump to forward somersault onto a 30 cm (1 ft) crashmat. As a precautionary measure when first performing this skill, it is recommended to use a 'Safety Belt'. (See next page for details on using a safety belt.)

Once the rider has developed the spatial (kinaesthetic) awareness to land correctly, the safety belt can be removed.

Progression #5: Forward somersault onto a crashmat:

After mastering the learning progressions, the rider should have no difficulty in performing a forward somersault from a short 5 m (16 ft) approach run. When doing the forward somersault from an approach run, the mini-tramp should be placed back in the normal position (not reversed as it was when jumping from a raised surface). Riders can also progress by using an air-board instead of a mini-tramp for take-off. A safety belt should also be used when first performing the skill from an approach run using either a mini-tramp or air-board.

Skill learning and training methods

Forward Somersault (continued)

USING A SAFETY BELT

A safety belt provides some protection for under or over rotation on landing.

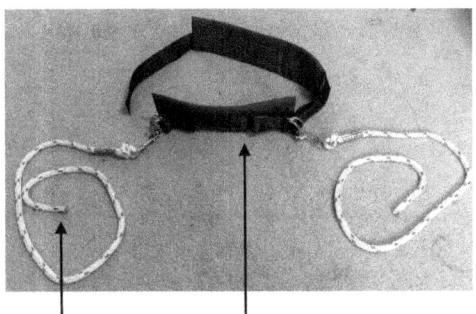

Swivel eye snap bolt | D-rings | 12 mm (1/2 in) polyester ropes | Padded adjustable belt

It is a simple inexpensive item of equipment that provides some protection from injury during the initial learning phase for aerial skills that involve rotation, such as dive rolls and somersaulting. Qualified instructors should be experienced in safety belt use. A safety belt requires two people to operate. Do some lead-up activity to enable the rider and any assistant to become familiar with the use of the safety belt before doing a dive roll or forward somersault in a safety belt for the first time.

Lead-up activity wearing a safety belt: tuck jump:

Forward Somersault (continued)

Forward somersault, 5 m (16 ft) approach run, from air-board using a safety belt:

Forward somersault, 5 m (16 ft) approach run, from air-board unassisted:

Key points:
- Once the rider can perform the forward somersault consistently in the safety belt with the instructor and assistant following the movement sequence—without having to apply tension on the ropes—the safety belt can be removed.
- Ensure that the head is neutral and looking forward at the point of take-off (not looking down towards the mat) and the arms in the brace position.
- Remember not to grab the shins during the somersault and to stay in an open tuck position.
- Do some practice wearing protective clothing in preparation for more advanced activities.
- Riders should be able to perform the forward somersault with confidence and consistency from a 5 m (16 ft) approach jog, using both a mini-tramp and an air-board, before progressing to more advanced somersault activities.

Forward Somersault (continued)

EXAMPLES OF SKILL PROGRESSION ACTIVITIES:

Forward somersault from mini-tramp to crashmat:

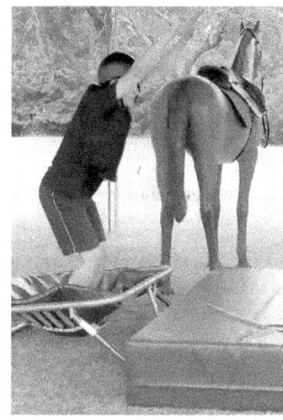

Forward somersault from mini-tramp to crashmat + forward roll:

Key points:

- After landing feet-first from the forward somersault with the arms in the brace position, continue into a forward roll.
- Be careful not to 'over rotate' the forward somersault and miss the feet-first landing position. Riders should gradually progress so that their momentum continues into the forward roll after landing from the somersault.
- When continuing into the forward roll, the head should be tucked in and not impact the mats or the ground during the forward roll.

Forward Somersault (continued)

Forward somersault to landing mat using an air-board:

Forward somersault to landing mat + forward roll using an air-board:

Key points:
- The above progression requires the same skills as those performed using a mini-tramp, except that an air-board is used for take-off.
- Using an air-board will allow the rider to gradually increase the speed of approach from a jog to a run—increasing from 5 to 10 m (16 to 33 ft) and then to a faster 20 m (66 ft) approach run.
- If a rider is having difficulties in performing the forward somersault correctly, experiences a loss of skill, has had a significant break in training, or is returning from injury, then it is important to go back and repeat the basic activities and skill progression on a crashmat before doing the more advanced activities.

VAULTING SKILLS AND SIMULATION ACTIVITIES

Police, soldiers, race car drivers, and helicopter pilots train to anticipate the strange behaviors they will encounter at the worst of times. They know that it's too late to learn those lessons in the midst of a crisis.

—Amanda Ripley (2009)
The Unthinkable: Who Survives When Disaster Strikes—and Why

Vaulting Skills

Developing skills in vaulting activities will assist riders to dismount and land in a variety of ways. The skills will provide a good means of improving fitness and will also assist in developing good landing habits and tumbling skills. Once learned, vaulting skills should enable riders to respond more intuitively in a fall. The skills detailed in this section are designed to simulate a number of landing directions and fall scenarios.

Vaulting skills are also a prerequisite for some more advanced simulation activities such as simulation exercises using a replica horse and a forward dive over a jumps obstacle.

The standard equipment for learning vaulting skills includes an air-board or mini-tramp for take-off and a vinyl-covered 4-section foam vaulting box. Each section is 30 cm (1 ft) high, so the height can be adjusted for rider age, skill level and progression.

Index for Vaulting Skills	Page
Straddle Vault Activities	118
Flank Vault Activities	120
Dive Roll Over a Vaulting Box	123

Straddle Vault Activities

Height progression:	Surface progression:	Speed progression:
Moderate High	Crashmat Landing mat Tumbling mat Grass/turf	Low Moderate

Prerequisites: Aerial skills using an air-board, including jump, land, and roll.

Learning progression: Straddle vault over 60 cm (2 ft) vaulting box from a standing start:

  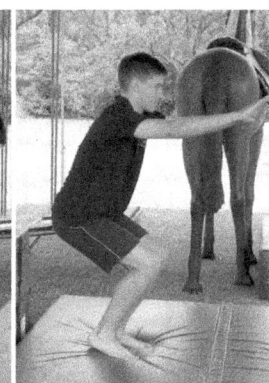

Key points:

- Take-off with a slight forward lean and place hands on the far end of the vaulting box, with legs in a straddle position.
- Push-off the vaulting box and bring the feet together and the arms into the brace position for landing.
- Bend the knees approximately 90-degrees on landing to absorb the impact force.
- After mastering this learning progression, the vaulting box height can be increased to 90 cm (3 ft) using a short approach run, and then to 120 cm (4 ft) height from a longer approach run.

REMINDER: Foot position on take-off from an air-board.

 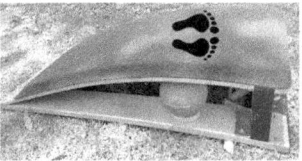 

Straddle Vault Activities (continued)

Straddle vault over 120 cm (4 ft) vaulting box:

Key points:
- Use a crashmat for each new progression, and once mastered progress to a landing mat.
- Use a 5 m (16 ft) approach run when learning, and then gradually increase the length and speed of the approach run.
- If the approach run is too slow, the rider will have difficulty in clearing the vaulting box during the straddle vault. Increase the length and speed of the approach run if required.

PROGRESSION: Once the straddle vault is performed well on a vaulting box height of 120 cm (4 ft), progression activities can include:

- increasing the vault box height to 150 cm (5 ft), by placing the 120 cm (4 ft) vaulting box on 30 cm (1 ft) of tumbling mats—6 × 5 cm (2 in) mats;
- progression to harder landing surfaces from a crashmat to a landing mat and then to tumbling mats;
- gradually increasing the approach run speed and distance to 20 m (66 ft); and
- landing followed by forward or sideways roll, particularly when increasing the speed of the approach run.

Straddle vault + forward roll: 120 cm (4 ft) vault box to landing mat:

Flank Vault Activities		
Height progression: Moderate High	**Surface progression:** Crashmat Landing mat Tumbling mat Grass/turf	**Speed progression:** Low Moderate

Prerequisites: Aerial skills using an air-board, including jump, land, and roll.

Learning progression: Flank vault over 90 cm (3 ft) vaulting box from a standing start:

Key points:

- Use a crashmat when learning the flank vault.
- Place one hand on each side of the vaulting box.
- Jump from the air-board (or alternatively a mini-tramp can be used) and swing the legs up and over the vaulting box landing side on to the vaulting box.
- When travelling over the box in a prone position, the body shape should be straight rather than piked.
- Learn the flank vault on both sides: i.e. land with the right shoulder adjacent to the box and also practice facing the other direction, landing with the left shoulder adjacent to the box.

Progress by adding a short two or three step jog and jump from the air-board or a mini-tramp before placing hands on the box. Once this progression is mastered, increase the box height to 120 cm (4 ft) and increase the approach run to about 5 m (16 ft).

Vaulting skills and simulation activities

Flank Vault Activities (continued)

Flank vault over 120 cm (4 ft) vaulting box:

Key points:

- Use a 5 m (16 ft) approach run when learning and gradually increase the length and speed of approach run.
- Adjust the air-board or mini-tramp position as required. Generally it should be at least 30 to 60 cm (1 to 2 ft) back from the vaulting box depending on the speed of the approach run to allow for some 'flight time' before placing the hands on the box.
- The body position should be straight, not piked, as the legs swing over the box.
- Use a crashmat for landing when first learning or progressing.
- Once mastered on one side, the flank vault should be learned and practiced on the other side.

Flank vault over 120 cm (4 ft) vaulting box, opposite side:

Flank Vault Activities (continued)

Flank vault + sideways roll, 120 cm (4 ft) vaulting box to landing mat:

Flank vault + ¼ turn, followed by backward roll, 90 cm (3 ft) vaulting box:

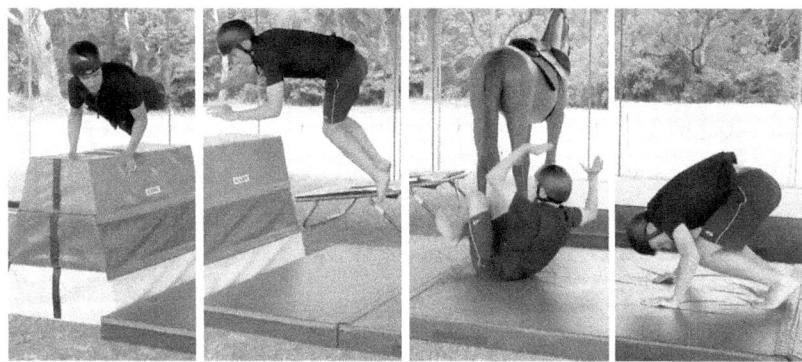

REMINDER:

When doing a backward roll, swing arms backward strongly to reduce the impact force on the head and neck and maintain a tuck position. The backward roll should be mastered as a stand-alone skill before including it in any combination activities.

Dive Roll Over Vaulting Box

Height progression:	Surface progression:	Speed progression:
Moderate	Crashmat	Low
High	Landing mat	Moderate

Prerequisites: Basic aerial skills using a mini-tramp and an air-board. Dive roll from 10 m (33 ft) approach run (moderate speed) using an air-board to a landing mat. Standing dive roll from a height of 120 cm (4 ft) to a crashmat. Riders should be able to confidently perform a dive roll in various situations unassisted before progressing to dive roll over an obstacle such as a vaulting box.

Dive roll over 60 cm (2 ft) vaulting box to crashmat using a mini-tramp:

Key points:
- Use a crashmat for landing when first introducing obstacles.
- The rider should be competent in performing the dive roll in the same situation at the required height before introducing the obstacle.
- Riders should not need to change their dive roll technique when performing the skill over an obstacle.
- Commence using a low height obstacle such as a 60 cm (2 ft) vaulting box.
- After learning to dive roll over a 60 cm (2 ft) height, progress to greater heights as required.

Dive roll over 120 cm (4 ft) vaulting box to crashmat:

Fall Simulation Activities

Simulation activities range from simple exercises that can be performed without any specialised equipment to advanced activities which include specialised equipment. Simulation is a great way to prepare for real situations that cannot be practically or safely reproduced at will.

Simulations are most effective when they can approximate a real situation as closely as possible. However, there is always a difference between a simulation and a real situation. Accordingly, qualified instructors should be mindful of providing some variety in simulated experiences in order to enable the rider to respond more intuitively in a fall scenario that may not always precisely match the training environment.

Index for Fall Simulation Activities	Page
Letting Go of the Reins and Brace Position	125
Replica Horse Simulations	127
Bicycle Simulation—Forward Dive Roll at Speed	130
Mechanical Horse Simulations	137

Vaulting skills and simulation activities

Letting Go of the Reins and Brace Position		Safe to do unsupervised
Height progression: Low, Moderate	**Surface progression:** Tumbling mat, Grass/turf	**Speed progression:** N/A

Prerequisites: Nil

This is a very basic simulation exercise that all riders can do regardless of skill or fitness level. It can be included in warm-up activities and should also be included in pre-ride safety routines. Letting go of the reins is not intuitive for riders and therefore it must be trained. On recognition that a fall is inevitable, it is important that riders have developed the skill to quickly let go of the reins. When practicing basic skills from a standing start, riders can commence in a simulated riding position, move the arms quickly into the brace position, and also perform this simulation in combination with other activities.

Warm-up activity: riding position to the brace position:

Warm-up activity: riding position, brace position, and then forward roll:

Key points:

- The arm movement should be quick with muscle tension—strong arms.
- Fingers should be together and hands turned in at approximately 45-degrees.
- Perform this skill in a variety of ways to facilitate skill transfer.

Letting Go of the Reins and Brace Position (Continued)

From kneeling on 60 cm (2 ft) height, brace position to forward roll:

From riding position on a 30 cm (1 ft) height with reins in hand, brace position then forward fall:

Key points:

- This can be varied by simulating the forward fall movement before letting go of the reins.
- A qualified instructor can also initiate the fall movement, by tipping the platform.
- This skill can be practiced with a forward roll and also with a sideways shoulder roll.
- The head should not impact the landing surface or the grass/turf when doing this exercise.

Vaulting skills and simulation activities

Replica Horse Simulations

Height progression:	Surface progression:	Speed progression:
High Advanced	Crashmat Landing mat Tumbling mat Grass/turf	Low Moderate

Prerequisites: A variety of simulation activities can be performed with a replica horse, from emergency dismount practice to vaulting skills and dive roll. The prerequisites required will depend on the activity being performed. Work with a qualified instructor to develop the appropriate prerequisite skills for the simulation activity being performed. The replica horse shown below is approximately 1.6 m (5.2 ft) or 16 hands at the withers—an average horse height. The hooves are anchored to the ground.

Emergency dismount practice onto grass/turf: (letting go of the reins)	Safe to do unsupervised* once mastered * on a replica horse

Key points:

- Start in riding position with feet in the stirrups.
- Quickly remove feet from the stirrups.
- Swing the leg strongly backward on the opposite side of the dismount to clear the back of the horse.
- Push away while letting go of the reins to land clear of the horse.
- Bend the knees and put the arms in the brace position when landing.
- Quickly move clear of the horse on landing.

The emergency dismount can be progressed by adding a roll in different directions on landing. The rider should be able to perform the basic rolling techniques from a platform height of 1.2 m (4 ft) onto grass/turf as a prerequisite. This is an important skill for riders, so they can quickly do an emergency dismount, if needed.

Replica Horse Simulations (continued)

Flank vault over replica horse from a standing start:

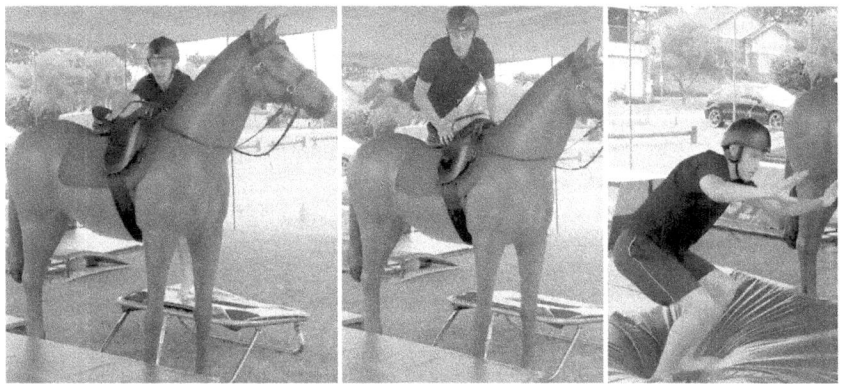

Key points:

- The flank vault should be mastered on the vaulting box before progression to a replica horse.
- Start from a standing position on the mini-tramp, holding the reins in each hand with the hands resting on the saddle.
- Do two or three preliminary bounces followed by the flank vault to finish in landing position.
- When first doing this skill, use a crashmat for the landing surface.
- Practice the skill on both sides, by shifting the mini-tramp and crashmat to the opposite side of the horse.

Flank vault over replica horse from a 5 m (16 ft) approach run:

Vaulting skills and simulation activities 129

Replica Horse Simulations (continued)

Dive roll over replica horse:

Prerequisite: Before performing this simulation exercise, the rider should be able to confidently and consistently perform a dive roll at a height of greater than 1.6 m (5 ft) above ground level. The rider should also have mastered a dive roll over a foam vaulting box at a similar height.

Dive roll mini-tramp to crashmat being performed at >1.6 m (5 ft):

Dive roll over replica horse to crashmat from an approach run:

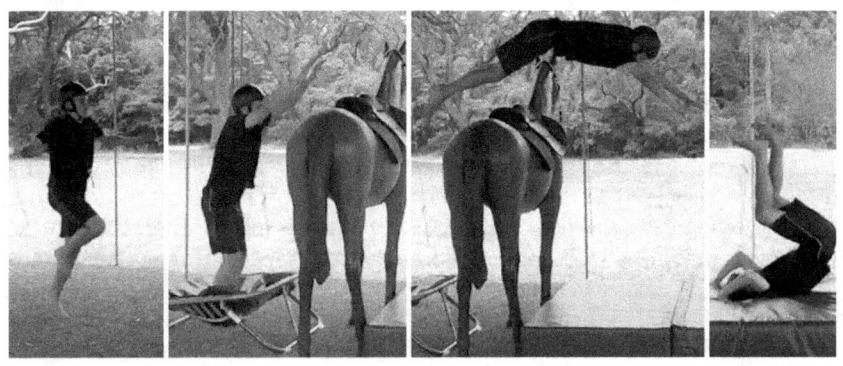

Bicycle Simulation—Forward Dive Roll at Speed

Height progression: Moderate	Surface progression: Crashmat Landing mat	Speed progression: Moderate High Advanced

Prerequisites: Dive roll from a fast 15 to 20 m (50 to 66 ft) approach run using an air-board. Progression activities #1 to #4.

This simulation exercise will develop the rider's skill in executing a dive roll technique in a forward head-first fall at speed—such as when a horse trips or breaks down suddenly or where a horse impacts a jumps obstacle and goes into a rotational fall. The body position and technique required for performance of the bicycle simulation is very similar to that required if a rider is propelled forward to the ground head-first. Mastering this skill will significantly reduce the risk of catastrophic injury for riders who are engaged in horse riding activities at speed or where the rider is engaged in higher-risk jumps activities.

EQUIPMENT SET-UP: A modified BMX or mountain-style bicycle is used for this simulation exercise, with a small platform securely fixed to the frame allowing the rider to simulate their normal riding position. The handlebars should be padded.

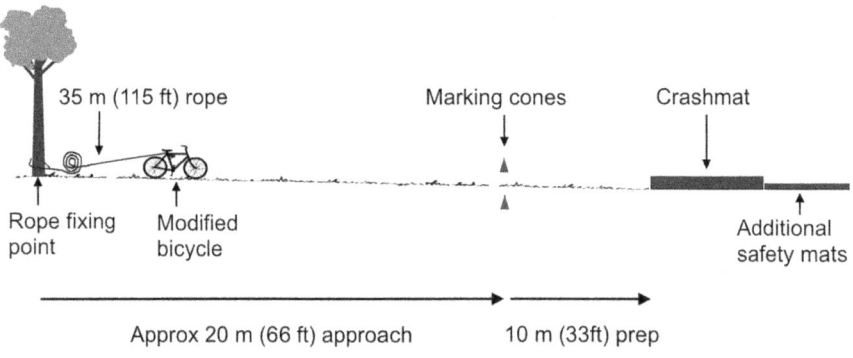

This simulation exercise should be conducted on a grass surface that is suitable for riding a bicycle. The surface should not be too soft or the grass too long as it will be difficult for the rider to build and maintain momentum. There needs to be a fixing point available for attachment of the rope, such as a tree, post, or tow point of a vehicle. The ground should also have a slight downward slope so the horizontal speed can be maintained when the rider transfers their feet from the pedals to the riding platform. If too much speed is lost following the 20 m (66 ft) approach, the rider may become unbalanced during the 10 m (33 ft) prep phase. The 35 m (115 ft) rope allows for a total approach distance of 30 m (100 ft), plus some additional length for securing the rope to a fixing point. Before the rope is secured to the bicycle, ensure that it is not tangled and will easily unfold.

Vaulting skills and simulation activities

Bicycle Simulation—Forward Dive Roll at Speed (continued)

Progression #1: From riding position, fall forward to standing dive roll from a 60 cm (2 ft) block to crashmat:

The rider should already have learned this skill and be proficient at performing a dive roll, including a dive roll from a fast approach run. This progression is just a refresher, to become familiar with the environment and to reinforce the initial movement sequence of letting go of the handle bars.

Key points:

- Wear comfortable sports shoes when doing bicycle simulation activities.
- When in the riding position for bicycle simulation activities, have the hands positioned as if hanging on to the handlebars, rather than simulating hanging on to the reins.
- Jump forward into the dive roll with head tucked in between arms at the point of impact with the mat.
- Once learned, bicycle simulation skills can also be performed wearing full riding uniform. This will further improve the rider's ability to transfer the skill in an emergency.

Bicycle Simulation—Forward Dive Roll at Speed (continued)

Progression #2: Practice riding the bicycle and moving feet from the pedals to the riding platform without the rope attached to the bike. This is a preparation drill to ensure that the rider is; 1) riding at a good speed; and 2) able to quickly transfer their feet from the pedals to the platform when passing through the marker cones. Perform this activity without the rope attached to the bike.

Pedalling to increase speed:

Transfer the feet to the riding platform after passing through the marker cones. The rider should transfer their feet to the platform while seated, then stand:

The rider should be balanced when reaching the crashmat position:

Vaulting skills and simulation activities

Bicycle Simulation—Forward Dive Roll at Speed (continued)

Key points: (Progression #2)

- When first learning this skill, aim to achieve a speed of about 15 km/h (9 mph), which is equivalent to a fast run, but not a full-speed sprint.
- The rider should not transfer their feet from the pedals to the riding platform too soon (before passing through the marker cones), as it may result in too much loss of speed during the final 10 m (33 ft) before reaching the crashmat position.
- After a few practice trials, the rider should be able to transfer their feet to the platform with about 5 m (16 ft) to spare before reaching the crashmat position.
- Progression #2 should be performed with the mats apart—not riding over the top of any mats—and can be practiced at the same time as Progression #1.
- At the point of reaching the crashmat position, the rider should have enough speed to travel in a straight line and maintain balance (not wobbling from side-to-side).

Progression #3: Forward dive roll from an air-board using a safety belt:

The rider should already have mastered the skill of performing a dive roll from an air-board and a fast approach run. If this has not been practiced recently, practice this skill before doing Progression #3. The purpose of this progression is; 1) to enable the rider to become accustomed to wearing a safety belt while doing a dive roll; and 2) to enable the two spotters (qualified instructor + assistant) to practice the approach run and ensure that they can support the rider as required during the dive roll.

Key points:

- Use a slower approach run initially and then increase to a faster approach run.
- The spotters should be able to keep up with the rider—not lag behind.
- The spotters should follow the rider through the movement sequence and only provide physical support to the rider as required—the rider should be able to perform the dive roll uninhibited.

Bicycle Simulation—Forward Dive Roll at Speed (continued)

Progression #4: Bicycle simulation—using a safety belt:

After the rider and spotters have mastered Progression #1 to #3, attach the rope to the bicycle, put the crashmat and additional safety mats in place, and perform the skill with the spotters supporting the rider through the movement sequence as required. Allow a small gap of about 20 cm (8 in) between the crashmat and the front wheel of the bicycle when the rope is fully unfolded—the rope will stretch when it becomes taut at speed.

Key points:
- The spotters need to remain adjacent to the rider and not lag behind. This requires the spotters to run fast and the rider to pace their speed accordingly. Do a trial run in the safety belt, without the bicycle rope attachment or mats in place, to establish the correct speed before first performing this skill with the rope attachment and mats.
- The rider should not jump from the riding platform but allow their momentum to carry them forward when the rope becomes taut.
- On recognition of the halt to bicycle momentum, the response action is; 'let go of the handlebars' (L); move the arms into 'the brace position' (B); 'land using dive roll technique' (L) and; 'tuck-and-roll' (T) following impact with the mat. This is the same response action required for a forward head-first horse riding fall.

BRACE!
Let go of reins   Brace position
⇨ (L)—(B)
              ↘
               (L)—(T) ⇨
              Land Tuck and roll
ROLL!

- The rider should maintain an open tuck position as the momentum carries them forward and not relax or allow their body shape to become completely stretched out.
- This progression with the safety belt should be repeated until the skill can be performed consistently over many repetitions.
- Do not feel compelled to remove the safety belt until confident to do so.

Bicycle Simulation—Forward Dive Roll at Speed (continued)

Bicycle simulation—forward dive roll at speed to crashmat:

Once the rider can perform the skill consistently well in the safety belt and with the spotters following the rider's movement but not providing any physical assistance to perform the skill, the safety belt can be removed.

Key points:
- When performing the skill without the safety belt, the rider can gradually increase the approach speed.
- Transfer the feet from the pedals to the platform while seated when passing the marking cones (but not before), then stand.
- The rider should, at the time of bicycle halt, let go of the handlebars but not jump from the platform. The rider should allow their momentum to carry them forward over the handle bars.
- After releasing the handlebars, the body shape should remain in an open tuck position, moving the arms into the brace position.

SAFETY NOTE: In the event of something unexpected happening—such as the rider losing balance or landing in a prone direction that may prevent the rider from doing the dive roll—the rider should remain in a tuck position, with arms in the brace position. It is likely that the rider will impact the ground/mat in a 4-point landing position.

Bicycle Simulation—Forward Dive Roll at Speed (continued)

FURTHER PROGRESSION:

After practicing the bicycle simulation—forward dive roll at speed—riders should find that the skill becomes easy to execute and any fear that they may have had should subside. Once the skill is performed consistently and confidently, further progression can be achieved by transitioning from crashmat to landing mat and then gradually increasing the approach speed. The bicycle should be well maintained and inspected before each days use.

Bicycle simulation—forward dive roll at speed to landing mat:

Bicycle simulation—forward dive roll + roll at increased speed to landing mat

Key points:
- As the approach speed increases, the rider will still have some momentum after completing the dive roll. Riders should allow their momentum to continue by remaining tucked and continuing into additional rolls until coming to a complete rest. This will enable the rider to develop the habit of correct response action in a real fall scenario at speed.
- When practicing a lot of rolling skills in one session (particularly after a break from training), it is likely that riders may begin to feel some nausea or dizziness. If this happens, discontinue with rolling activities and do some other activity for the remainder of the session that does not require rolling.

Vaulting skills and simulation activities

Mechanical Horse Simulations

Height progression:	Surface progression:	Speed progression:
N/A	Air-mattress	N/A

Prerequisites: Basic aerial and rolling skills.

Mechanical horse simulations should only be done under the supervision of an experienced operator and qualified fall safety instructor.

The skills that have been detailed so far, once learned, will provide some protection for riders in various fall scenarios. To further develop skill levels, include additional simulation activities where safe and practical to do so. A mechanical rodeo bull (with horse attachment) offers an opportunity to practice additional fall simulation activities and add an element of surprise—where the rider cannot anticipate the precise nature and/or timing of a fall scenario. Because the mechanical horse is spinning and/or bucking but not travelling at speed, it can be best used to simulate sideways emergency dismount and sideways fall scenarios, but not a forward fall at speed.

Emergency dismount practice from a mechanical horse:

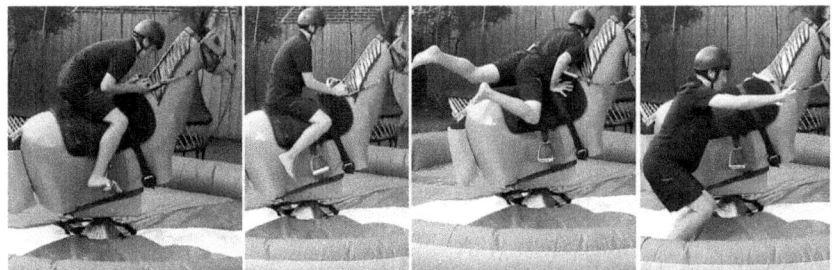

Key points:

- Quickly take the feet out of the stirrups. (If using stirrups, they should be padded safety stirrups with only the ball/front of the foot in the stirrups).
- Let go of the reins and quickly swing one leg backward and over the hindquarters while pushing away from the horse.
- Bend the knees, landing in the brace position, and immediately move clear of the horse.
- If landing at an angle, continue into a roll and maintain tuck position with arms in the brace position.
- Practice an emergency dismount on both sides of the horse until it can be performed quickly and landing clear of the horse.
- Once mastered from both sides of a stationary mechanical horse, this skill can be practiced with the mechanical horse moving.
- The operator should stop the mechanical horse as the rider is dismounting.

Mechanical Horse Simulations (continued)

Sideways practice fall to air-mattress—arms in the brace position:

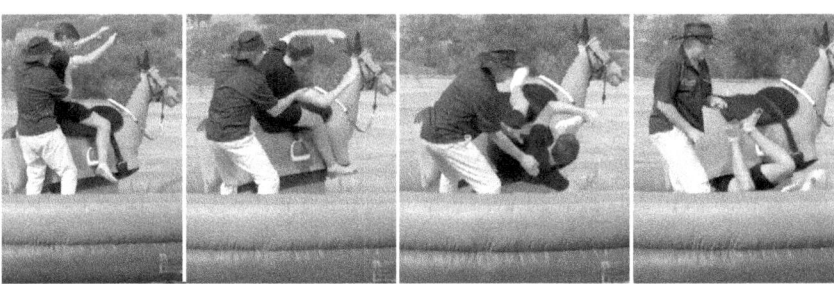

This is a prerequisite skill that should be done before riders fall from a moving mechanical horse. It should be done with qualified instructor assistance. Riders who are not proficient or confident in doing a practice fall with assistance, should not progress to the sideways fall from a moving mechanical horse. It is performed with a qualified instructor pulling the rider off the stationary mechanical horse and guiding the rider's fall so they do not land head-first.

Key points:
- Do not use the stirrups for this exercise.
- Move the arms into the brace position and maintain muscle tension in the arms.
- During the fall, the rider should maintain a tuck position, with head-in and landing with muscle tension in a tuck position.
- There should be minimal impact of the head on the air cushion—the arms in the brace position should protect the head and neck from most of the impact with the air-mattress.
- The rider may begin to roll as they land and also may roll against the side wall of the air-mattress. The rider should not relax their arms or body position as they begin to roll or impact the side wall of the air-mattress.
- Practice the sideways fall on both sides.
- The exercise can be varied by holding the reins and then letting go of the reins as the rider falls.
- Spectators or other riders awaiting their turn should stand clear of the sidewall of the air-mattress to avoid getting kicked or hit by a rider who may be impacting the sidewall of the air-mattress.
- Place a safety mat at the entrance to the air-mattress in case the rider falls and rolls through the entrance gap. Riders or spectators should not stand on this safety mat while a rider is having their turn.

Vaulting skills and simulation activities

Mechanical Horse Simulations (continued)

Sideways fall from mechanical horse with buck-spin:

Prerequisite: Sideways practice fall from a stationary mechanical horse.

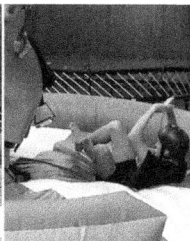

Key points:

- This skill can be performed without stirrups, or alternatively with feet in the stirrups. The stirrups must be padded safety stirrups.
- If using stirrups, only place the ball/front of the foot in the stirrups, not the full foot in the stirrups. This will minimise risk of the feet getting caught in the stirrups when falling.
- When falling, the rider should let go of the reins, and snap the arms into the brace position.
- Maintain a rigid tuck position with arms in the brace position during the fall.
- Allow the momentum to continue into a roll in any direction on impact with the air cushion.
- The rider should not relax their arms or body shape until they come completely to rest on the air cushion.

NOTE:

The operator of the mechanical horse should be experienced and trained in its operation and safety procedures. This means that the mechanical horse's movement (buck-spin) will be stopped immediately on the rider commencing their fall. The speed and difficulty level of the buck-spin should be varied to suit the rider's age, ability, and confidence level. Riders must not be forced to fall from the moving mechanical horse against their will and the speed and difficulty level should be agreed on with the rider before commencement.

Pre-ride Safety Routines

It is recommended that riders do some general warm-up exercises before each riding session. Guidelines for general warm-up are detailed in the section 'Warm-up and Conditioning Exercises'. Completion of a pre-ride safety routine is an important activity for all riders and will take only a couple of minutes after general warm-up exercises. Helmet and body protector (if worn during riding) should be worn when doing the pre-ride safety routine. It is recommended that neck exercises be completed immediately prior to the pre-ride safety routine as a part of the general warm-up activities. Neck exercises will take about two minutes and the pre-ride safety routine, once learned, will also take about two minutes. The benefits of doing general warm-up and a pre-ride safety routine are significant, and include:

- better physical and mental preparation for each day's riding,
- improved stress tolerance when force is applied to the neck,
- improved kinaesthetic awareness, which will support riding skills, and
- better retention of fall safety skills.

The pre-ride safety routine should be completed twice, with a short break in between each routine if desired. This routine should be varied periodically and it should only include skills that the rider has previously mastered. Work with your qualified instructor to assist in modifying the routine as new skills are developed.

The pre-ride safety routines detailed in this section are examples and can be performed as shown or modified as required to suit individual requirements. It is recommended that riders change or vary the pre-ride safety routine on a quarterly or six-monthly basis.

Index for Pre-ride Safety Routines	Page
Basic Pre-ride Routine #1	142
Basic Pre-ride Routine #2	144
Intermediate Pre-ride Routine	146
Advanced Pre-ride Routine #1	148
Advanced Pre-ride Routine #2	150

Basic Pre-ride Safety Routine #1		Safe to do unsupervised once mastered.
Height progression: N/A	**Surface progression:** Tumbling mat Grass/turf	**Speed progression:** N/A

Prerequisites: General warm-up and neck conditioning exercises. Wear helmet and body protector when doing the pre-ride safety routine.

STEP 1) From riding position, snap arms quickly into the brace position, then fall backward and complete rock and roll three times, standing after the third one and finishing in landing position.

Simulate hands holding the reins.	Strong arms with muscle tension.	Maintain a tight tuck with knees slightly apart moving the arms to rock.	Stand without using the hands.	Landing position, with muscle tension in the arms.

STEP 2) Kneel down, move the arms into riding position, snap to the brace position three times. Place the hands on the ground (directly under the shoulders), move into angry cat position and hold three seconds. Raise the knees off the ground to 4-point landing position and complete three push-ups maintaining a rigid body shape. Touch the head gently on the ground with each push-up, then stand.

Simulate hands holding the reins.	Strong arms with muscle tension.	Rounded back, push through the shoulders, head-in.	Move into 4-point landing position.	Touch the head on each push-up, maintain a rigid body shape.

Pre-ride safety routines

Basic Pre-ride Safety Routine #1 (continued)

STEP 3) Move into riding position and hold two seconds. Fall forward, move the arms quickly into the brace position and continue into a forward roll to landing position. Hold the landing position for two seconds, then stand.

Simulate hands holding the reins.	Strong arms with muscle tension.	Maintain a tight tuck position with knees slightly apart and back rounded.	Stand without using the hands, maintain the arms in the brace position.	Finish in landing position, with muscle tension in the arms.

STEP 4) Walk or jog one or two steps forward and then do a small jump with 45-degree turn left to 4-point landing position and continue into a sideways roll to landing position. Then stand. Repeat, except this time do a small jump with 45-degree turn right to 4-point landing position and continue into a sideways roll to landing position. Then stand and turn 180 degrees to face the opposite direction.

Small jump with 45-degree turn left to 4-point landing.	Continue into a sideways roll, hands turned slightly in, head between the arms.	Maintain tuck position, with the arms strong and in the brace position.	Jump with 45-degree turn right to 4-point landing position.	Continue into sideways roll, and finish in landing position.

REPEAT the full routine, STEP 1) to STEP 4) facing the opposite direction, excluding the neck exercises.

Basic Pre-ride Safety Routine #2		Safe to do unsupervised once mastered.
Height progression: N/A	**Surface progression:** Tumbling mat Grass/turf	**Speed progression:** N/A
Prerequisites: General warm-up and neck conditioning exercises. Wear helmet and body protector when doing the pre-ride safety routine.		

STEP 1) From riding position, snap the arms quickly into the brace position, then jump forward to feet-first landing, followed by a forward roll to stand.

Simulate hands holding the reins.	Strong arms with muscle tension.	Straight jump and land feet-first.	Continue into a forward roll.	Stand with the arms in the brace position.

STEP 2) Kneel down, move the arms into riding position, snap the arms to the brace position three times. Place the hands on the ground (directly under the shoulders), move into angry cat position and hold three seconds. Raise the knees off the ground to 4-point landing position and complete three push-ups maintaining a rigid body shape. Touch the head gently on the ground with each push-up, then stand.

Simulate hands holding the reins.	Strong arms with muscle tension.	Rounded back, push through the shoulders, head-in.	Move into 4-point landing position.	Touch the head on each push-up, maintaining a rigid body shape.

Pre-ride safety routines

Basic Pre-ride Safety Routine #2 (continued)

STEP 3) From 4-point landing position, push off with the feet into a forward roll to stand. Roll backward to candle position and then roll forward to stand. (Riders who have mastered a backward roll on grass/turf can do a full backward roll instead of the half roll backward to candle position.)

4-point landing position.	Push off into a forward roll.	Stand without using hands, with arms in the brace position.	Roll backward to candle—strong arm movement to protect the head/neck.	Roll forward to stand.

STEP 4) Walk or jog one or two steps forward and then do a small jump with 45-degree turn left to 4-point landing position and continue into a sideways roll to landing position. Then stand. Repeat, except this time do a small jump with 45-degree turn right to 4-point landing position and continue into a sideways roll to landing position. Then stand, turn 180 degrees to face the opposite direction.

Small jump with 45-degree turn left to 4-point landing position.	Continue into a sideways roll, hands turned slightly in, head between the arms.	Maintain tuck position, arms strong and in the brace position.	Jump with 45-degree turn right to 4-point landing.	Continue into a sideways roll, and finish in landing position.

REPEAT the full routine, STEP 1) to STEP 4) facing the opposite direction, excluding the neck exercises.

Intermediate Pre-ride Safety Routine		Safe to do unsupervised once mastered.
Height progression: N/A	**Surface progression:** Tumbling mat Grass/turf	**Speed progression:** N/A
Prerequisites: General warm-up and neck conditioning exercises. Wear helmet and body protector when doing the pre-ride safety routine.		

STEP 1) From riding position, snap the arms quickly into the brace position, then fall backward and complete a rock and roll three times. After the third one, roll forward to landing position.

Simulate hands holding the reins.	Strong arms with muscle tension.	Maintain a tight tuck position with knees slightly apart.	Stand with the arms in the brace position.	Landing position, with muscle tension in arms.

STEP 2) Backward roll to stand. (Substitute half backward roll to candle position, if the backward roll has not been mastered on a grass/turf surface.) Two or three steps run, single foot take-off and star jump, landing with feet together and continue into a forward roll to stand.

Move the arms back strongly to protect head and neck.	Backward roll and then stand.	Two or three steps run, single-foot take-off.	Star jump, land with feet together and continue into a forward roll.	Maintain the arms in the brace position when rolling to stand.

Pre-ride safety routines 147

Intermediate Pre-ride Safety Routine (continued)

STEP 3) Kneel down, move the arms into riding position, snap to the brace position three times. Place the hands on the ground (directly under the shoulders), move into angry cat position and hold three seconds. Raise the knees off the ground to 4-point landing position and complete three push-ups maintaining a rigid body shape. Touch the head gently on the ground with each push-up, then do a forward roll to stand.

Simulate hands holding the reins.	Strong arms with muscle tension.	Rounded back, push through the shoulders, head-in.	Move into 4-point landing position.	Touch the head on each push-up, maintain a rigid body shape. Then forward roll to stand.

STEP 4) Walk or jog one or two steps forward and then do a small jump with 45-degree turn left to 4-point landing position and continue into a sideways roll to landing position. Then stand. Repeat, except this time do a small jump with 45-degree turn right to 4-point landing position and continue into a sideways roll to landing position. Then stand, turn 180 degrees to face the opposite direction.

Small jump with 45-degree turn left to 4-point landing position.	Continue into a sideways roll, hands turned slightly in, head between the arms.	Maintain tuck position, with the arms strong and in the brace position.	Jump with 45-degree turn right to 4-point landing position.	Continue into a sideways roll, and finish in landing position.

REPEAT the full routine, STEP 1) to STEP 4) facing the opposite direction, excluding the neck exercises.

Advanced Pre-ride Safety Routine #1		Safe to do unsupervised once mastered.
Height progression: N/A	**Surface progression:** Tumbling mat Grass/turf	**Speed progression:** N/A

Prerequisites: General warm-up and neck conditioning exercises. Wear helmet and body protector when doing the pre-ride safety routine.

STEP 1) From riding position, snap arms quickly into the brace position, then lean forwards and do a standing dive roll to landing position.

Simulate hands holding the reins.	Snap the arms into the brace position.	Standing dive roll with some 'flight time'.	Roll with arms in the brace position.	Finish in landing position.

STEP 2) Step and reach forward, placing the hands down and swing one leg up and kick to handstand. Continue momentum into a forward roll.

   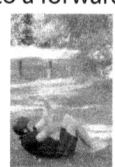 

Step and reach forward.	Move through handstand position.	Continue into a forward roll.	Forward roll.	Finish in landing position.

STEP 3) Kneel down, move the arms into riding position, snap to the brace position three times. Place hands on the ground and move into angry cat position. Raise the knees off the ground to 4-point landing position and complete three push-ups maintaining a rigid body shape. Touch the head gently with each push-up, then forward roll to stand. Turn 180 degrees.

Simulate hands holding the reins.	Strong arms with muscle tension.	Rounded back, push through the shoulders, head-in.	4-point landing position.	Three push-ups with rigid body shape, then forward roll to stand.

Pre-ride safety routines

Advanced Pre-ride Safety Routine #1 (continued)

STEP 4) Two or three steps jog, single-foot take-off with half turn, landing with the feet together and with backward momentum. Continue into a backward roll to landing position.

Two or three step jog and single foot take-off.	Two feet landing with backward momentum.	Continue into a backward roll.	Move arms back strongly to protect head and neck.	Finish in landing position.

STEP 5) Walk or jog one or two steps forward and then do a small jump with 45-degree turn left to 4-point landing position and continue into a sideways roll to landing position. Then stand. Repeat, except this time do a small jump with 45-degree turn right to 4-point landing position and continue into a sideways roll to landing position. Then stand, turn 180 degrees to face the opposite direction.

Small jump with 45-degree turn left to 4-point landing position.	Continue into a sideways roll, hands turned slightly in, head between the arms.	Maintain tuck position, the arms strong and in the brace position.	Jump with 45-degree turn right to 4-point landing position.	Continue into a sideways roll, and finish in landing position.

REPEAT the full routine, STEP 1) to STEP 5), facing the opposite direction, excluding the neck exercises.

Fall safety training for horse riders

Advanced Pre-ride Safety Routine #2		Safe to do unsupervised once mastered.
Height progression: N/A	**Surface progression:** Tumbling mat Grass/turf	**Speed progression:** N/A
Prerequisites: General warm-up and neck conditioning exercises. Wear helmet and body protector when doing the pre-ride safety routine.		

STEP 1) From riding position, snap the arms quickly into the brace position, then lean forwards and do a standing dive roll and finish in landing position.

Simulate hands holding the reins.	Strong arms with muscle tension.	Standing dive roll with some 'flight time'.	Roll with the arms in the brace position.	Finish in landing position.

STEP 2) Step and reach forward, placing the hands down and swing one leg up, and kick to handstand. Continue momentum into a forward roll to stand. Turn 180 degrees and face the opposite direction.

Step and reach forward.	Move through handstand position.	Continue into a forward roll.	Forward roll.	Half turn and face the opposite direction.

STEP 3) Fast run—approximately 10 m (33 ft)—jump with two-foot take-off into a dive roll and continue into a second forward roll (or sideways roll) to stand with the arms in the brace position.

Fast run.	Jump with two-feet take-off.	Dive roll.	Continue rolling into a second roll.	Stand with the arms in the brace position.

Advanced Pre-ride Safety Routine #2 (continued)

STEP 4) Kneel down, move the arms into riding position, snap to the brace position three times. Place the hands on the ground and move into 4-point landing position. Complete three push-ups maintaining a rigid body shape. Touch the head gently on the ground with each push-up. Stand, then roll backward to stand.

Simulate hands holding the reins.	Strong arms with muscle tension.	4-point landing position, head between the arms.	Three push-ups with rigid body shape, then stand.	Backward roll moving arms back strongly to protect the head and neck.

STEP 5) Walk or jog one or two steps forward and then do a small jump with 45-degree turn left to 4-point landing position and continue into a sideways roll to landing position. Then stand. Repeat, except this time do a small jump with 45-degree turn right to 4-point landing position and continue into a sideways roll to landing position. Then stand, turn 180 degrees to face the opposite direction.

Small jump with 45-degree turn left to 4-point landing position.	Continue into a sideways roll, hands turned slightly in, head between the arms.	Maintain tuck position, arms strong and in the brace position.	Jump with 45-degree turn right to 4-point landing position.	Continue into sideways roll, and finish in landing position.

REPEAT the full routine, STEP 1) to STEP 5), facing the opposite direction, excluding the neck exercises.

SKILLS ASSESSMENT

Skills assessment is a good way of measuring progress in any activity that requires skills development, particularly in sporting activities. The benefits of skills assessment are significant. At a personal level, skills assessment will enable riders to; measure and track their progress, develop strategies and set goals for improvement, make decisions on the amount and frequency of follow-up training, and reduce the risk of injury and downtime. It will also provide valuable information for qualified instructors to plan progression rates that are appropriate for each rider's ability, skill, and fitness level.

Measurement of rider skill levels and collection of other data will also enable administrators and safety professionals to allocate resources that may be needed for improved rider safety. Furthermore, the information obtained from skills assessment will enable research and development of additional evidence-based strategies to help improve injury outcomes for riders of all disciplines.

Rider fall safety training is predominantly skills-based training. However, rider fitness level is also important for reduced risk of injury in a fall. Riders will benefit from a regular fitness and exercise regime that is specific to their individual circumstances and riding activity. Apart from the fall safety skills and muscle conditioning exercises—such as neck exercises, push-ups in the 4-point landing position, and abdominal exercises—there are two fitness measures that will be beneficial to record at the time of skills assessment.

1. BODY MASS INDEX (BMI)

The science in relation to forces of impact demonstrates that the force of impact with the ground in a fall is directly proportional to body mass. An increase or decrease in rider weight (relative to their size and their muscle strength) will therefore increase or decrease the risk of injury in a fall. Because rider weight is not a relative measure, it is not useful in the absence of any other information. For example, a young rider will get heavier as they grow in height, but this does not necessarily mean that their risk of injury will increase. BMI is a relative measure that takes into account both height and weight and is therefore more useful.

$$BMI = \text{Body weight in kilograms} / (\text{Height in metres})^2$$

OR

$$BMI = \text{Body weight in pounds} \times 703 / (\text{Height in inches})^2$$

BMI ratings of between 18.5 and 25 are considered normal (World Health Organisation, 2000), with ratings under 18.5 considered underweight and 25.0 and over considered overweight. Because BMI does not measure body composition—muscle mass versus body fat—it should only be used as a general guideline. If BMI ratings are unexpectedly high or low, riders should consult a fitness instructor or medical professional for further advice. It is also worth noting that a lower BMI may not always be better. A very low BMI rating may indicate muscle wasting or a loss of muscle strength which may adversely affect riders' ability to protect themselves in a fall. Tracking changes to BMI over time will be more useful than a once-only measure. It is recommended that riders' height, weight, and BMI be recorded at the time of skills assessment.

2. SIMPLE REACTION TIME (SRT)

The time available for response action in a fall is very short, but fortunately within the capability of riders to respond in most falls providing they have been trained in how to respond. An important component of the overall response action is the time taken to react when a fall becomes inevitable. Anything that may affect a rider's simple reaction time, such as an illness, concussion or head injury, is a risk factor for riders and measurement of simple reaction time can help identify this risk. It is recommended that SRT be carried out at the commencement of the training program and also after any head injury. Measurement of simple reaction time can be easily done without any specialised equipment requiring only a 45 cm (18 in) ruler or a 60 cm (24 in) ruler for riders such as younger children who may have a slower SRT. The test should be carried out with both the rider and tester being seated.

Procedure:

- The tester holds the ruler so that it remains steady and positioned between the index finger and thumb of the rider's dominant hand. The top of the rider's thumb should be level with the 0 measure on the bottom of the ruler.
- The rider must catch the ruler as soon as possible after it begins to fall. The tester says 'ready', and then waits between one and five seconds to let go of the ruler. On each attempt, the tester should vary the wait time slightly.
- The tester releases the ruler and the rider catches the ruler between their index finger and thumb as fast as they can.
- Note the distance at the top of the rider's thumb after they grasp the ruler.
- Allow the rider two practice attempts to become familiar with the test.
- After the two practice attempts, perform the test three times and record the distance for the median value (ignoring the shortest and longest values).
- Calculate the SRT and record the result to the nearest millisecond.

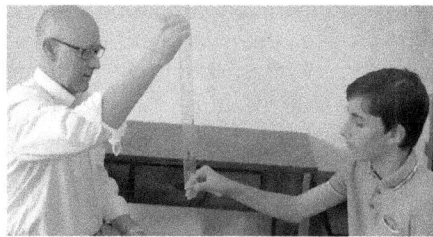
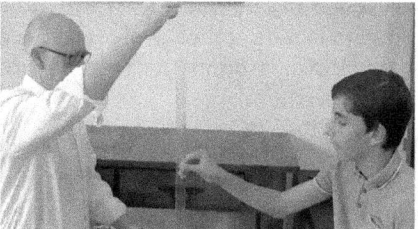

The following formula can be used to calculate SRT in milliseconds based on the drop distance:

SRT = [Square root (2 x distance / Gravity)] x 100

SRT = [Square root (2 x d / 9.8)] x 100

SRT for a drop distance of 20 cm = 202 ms

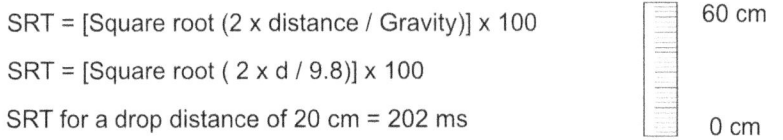

It is recommended that skills assessment be carried out after completion of a program of nine training sessions with the tenth session being used for skills assessment. The recommended duration of training sessions (excluding the time for equipment set-up) is

Age 7 to 11 years	1 hour
Age 12 to 16 years	1.5 hours
Age 17 years and over	2 hours

Most riders will improve their skill levels significantly over ten training sessions and this allows for repetition and refinement of basic skills so that a rider's initial response action in a fall becomes more intuitive. It may also be beneficial to carry out basic skills assessment during the fifth training session. Many of the basic skills are likely to be mastered after about four training sessions. Skills assessment can provide motivation to continue with further training and also enable qualified instructors to tailor subsequent training sessions and skills progression based on the assessment results.

The sample skills assessment form that follows provides examples of activities and can be modified to suit the age and skill level of the rider. Riders should not attempt a skill or progression for the first time when being assessed. Assessment should only include the skills and the level that have previously been mastered. For example, if a rider has only practiced a straight jump to feet-first landing, followed by a forward roll from a platform of 90 cm (3 ft) in the training sessions, they should only be assessed at this height and not at, say, 120+ cm (4+ ft).

The sample skills assessment matrix allows for recording of landing surface, height, and speed in addition to the skill proficiency rating. Riders should be assessed within the limits of their proficiency level. The use of a numerical rating system can enable the measurement of overall proficiency in fall safety skills and target areas for improvement.

A rider who performs a skill in accordance with all of the key points as detailed in the skill learning sections of this book can be rated 10. A rider who is performing a skill in a safety belt can be rated as 3 (partial achievement) for that skill.

Rating Method for Fall Safety Skills Assessment

0 = not attempted, 1 = attempted but not achieved, 3 = partial achievement, 6 = basic proficiency, 8 = good skill level with some room for improvement, and 10 = high standard.

Landing surface can be recorded as crashmat (C), landing mat (L), tumbling mat (T), and grass/turf (G).

For jumps from a raised platform and vaulting skills, the height can be recorded. For ease of reference, use the height of the take-off surface or height of the vaulting box. For aerial skills, such as straight jump or dive roll using a mini-tramp, the height can be estimated from the difference between the rider's centre of gravity (in the middle part of the body) and the landing surface.

Speed can be estimated and recorded as 'N/A' (standing start), 'Low' (jog), 'Moderate' (run), and 'High' (fast sprint).

SKILLS ASSESSMENT for: _____ **Date:** _____

Height: _____ Weight: _____ BMI: _____ Dist.: _____ SRT (ms): _____

SKILL	Surface	Height	Speed	Assess.
Basics				
Riding position to the brace position	N/A	N/A	N/A	
Riding position to 4-point landing	N/A	N/A	N/A	
4-point landing position + 3 push-ups	N/A	N/A	N/A	
Forward roll		N/A	N/A	
Sideways roll—left		N/A	N/A	
Sideways roll—right		N/A	N/A	
Egg roll × 3—left		N/A	N/A	
Egg roll × 3—right		N/A	N/A	
Dive roll drill		N/A	N/A	
Backward roll down incline		N/A	N/A	
Straight jump to landing position			N/A	
Star jump to landing position			N/A	
Tuck jump to landing position			N/A	
Jump ½ turn to landing position			N/A	
Emergency dismount—left			N/A	
Emergency dismount—right			N/A	
Jump land + forward roll			N/A	
Jump, 4-point landing + side roll—left			N/A	
Jump, 4-point landing + side roll—right			N/A	
Jump ½ turn land + backward roll			N/A	
Handstand roll		N/A	N/A	
Basic pre-ride safety routine		N/A	N/A	
Progression				
Run + straight jump + forward roll				
Run + star jump + forward roll				
Run + tuck jump + forward roll				
Run + 4-point landing + side roll—left				
Run + 4-point landing + side roll—right				
Run + jump ½ turn + backward roll				
Straddle vault + forward roll				
Flank vault left + sideways roll				
Flank vault right + sideways roll				
Flank vault ¼ turn + backward roll				
Standing dive roll from low height			N/A	
Dive roll at height				
Run + dive roll at speed + roll				
4-point landing + multiple incline roll				
Intermediate pre-ride safety routine		N/A	N/A	
Total:				

REFERENCES

ABC News. (2016) 'Michelle Payne lost memory of winning Melbourne Cup in Mildura fall from horse', [www.abc.net.au/news/2016-06-10/michelle-payne-lost-memory-of-winning-melbourne-cup/7500738]. Accessed Jun 2016.

Balakrishnan, G., Uppinakufru, G., Singh, G., Bangera, S., Raghavendra, A., Thangavel, D. (2014) 'A comparative study on visual choice reaction time for different colors in females', Neurology Research International, vol. 2014, Article ID 301473, 5 pages.

Bertelson, P. (1967) 'The time course of preparation', Quarterly Journal of Experimental Psychology, vol. 19, pp. 272–279.

British Equestrian Vaulting. (2011) 'A Brief History of Vaulting', [www.vaulting.org.uk/information/history-of-vaulting]. Accessed Jan 2016.

British Racing School. (2014). 'Fall Training', [www.brs.org.uk/courses/fall-train/]. Accessed Jun 2016.

Corbin, C., Le Masauier, G. and McConnell, K. (2014) *Fitness for Life*, 6th Edition, Human Kinetics, Champaign, Illinois, p. 212.

Cowley, S., Bowman M. and Lawrance M. (2007) 'Injuries in the Victorian thoroughbred racing industry', British Journal of Sports Medicine, vol. 41 (10), pp. 639-634.

Cripps, R. A. (2000) 'Horse-related injury in Australia'. Australian Injury Prevention Bulletin 24, Research Centre for Injury Studies, Flinders University, AIHW, Cat. No. INJ26.

Deng, S., Javed, S., Tan, J., and Weng, N. (2006) 'Fingertip reaction time', The Physics Factbook.

O'Brien, D. (2016) 'Look before you leap: what are the obstacles to risk calculation in the equestrian sport of eventing?' Animals, vol.6 (13), doi:10.3390.

Der, G. and Deary, I. (2006) 'Age and sex differences in reaction time in adulthood: results from the United Kingdom Health and Lifestyle Survey', Psychology and Aging, vol. 21(1), pp. 62–73.

Exploratorium. (2016) [www.exploratorium.edu/baseball/biobaseball.html]. Accessed Jun 2016.

FEI (2015) 'FEI Eventing Risk Management Seminar—Madrid (ESP) Report', Updated: 13-Mar-2015.

FEI (2016) 'FEI Eventing Risk Management Seminar—Brussels (BEL) (DRAFT) Report', Updated: 8-Mar-2016.

Foote, C.E., Gibson, T.J. and McGauran, P.J. (2014) 'Evaluation of safety vests—health and safety in Australian racing', Rural Industries Research and Development Corporation, Publication No. 14/037.

Finch, C.F. and Watt G.M. (1996) 'Locking the Stable Door: Preventing Equestrian Injuries', Monash University Accident Research Centre, Report #103, 1996.

Fischman, M., Christina, R. and Vercruyssen, M. (1982) 'Retention and transfer of motor skills: a review for the practitioner', Quest, vol. 33(2), pp. 181–194.

Gavkare, A., Nanaware, N. and Surdi, A. (2013) 'Auditory reaction time and whole body reaction time in athletes', Indian Medical Gazette, June 2013, pp. 214–219.

Gladwell, M. (2005) Blink: *The Power of Thinking without Thinking*, Penguin Books, London, pp. 50, 114, 143.

Hitchens, P., Blizzard, C., Jones, G., Day, L. and Fell, J. (2009) 'The incidence of race-day jockey falls in Australia, 2002–2006', Medical Journal of Australia, vol. 190 (2), pp. 83–86.

Hitchens, P., Blizzard, C., Jones, G., Day, L. and Fell, J. (2010) 'Predictors of race-day jockey falls in flat racing in Australia', Journal of Occupational and Environmental Medicine, vol. 67(10), pp. 693–698.

Hitchens, P., Blizzard, C., Jones, G., Day, L. and Fell, J. (2011) 'Are physiological attributes of jockeys predictors of falls? A pilot study', Supplementary table 1, British Medical Journal, BJM Open, doi:10.1136/bmjopen-2011-000142.

Hope, D., Bates, T., Dykiert, D., Der, G. and Deary, I. (2015) 'More symmetrical children have faster and more consistent choice reaction times', Developmental Psychology, vol. 51(4), pp. 524–532.

Jander, C. (2009) 'Study of improvements in international health protection standards for jockeys in the United Kingdom, Ireland, France and Germany, Fellowship Report by Dr Caron Bridget Jander', The Winston Churchill Memorial Trust of Australia.

Kosinski, R. (2008) 'A Literature Review on Reaction Time', Clemson University.

Lansing, R.N., Schwartz, E. and Lindsley, D.B. (1959) 'Reaction time and EEG activation under alerted and non-alerted conditions', Journal of Experimental Psychology, vol. 58, pp. 1–7.

Mason-Jones, D. (1997) *Akos Kovacs An Hungarian-Australian Odyssey*, Phillip Mathews Book Publishers, Sydney, p. 72.

Medical Equestrian Association. (2012). Gallery of Falls, [www.medequestrian.co.uk/gallery-falls/], Accessed Jun 2016.

Melnick, M. (1971) 'Effects of overlearning on the retention of a gross motor skill', Research Quarterly, vol. 42, pp. 60–69.

Mertz, H., Irwin A. and Prasad, P. (2003) 'Biomechanical and scaling bases for frontal and side impact assessment reference values', Stapp Car Crash Journal, vol. 47(Oct 2003), pp. 155-188.

Newell, K. and Shapiro, D. (1976). 'Variability of practice and transfer of training: some evidence toward a schema view of motor learning'. Journal of Motor Behavior, vol. 8:233-243.

Nylund, L (2016) 'Jockey, showjumping and cross-country rider fall times'. Unpublished review, 2016.

Northey, G. (2006) 'Interpreting human and horse interactions, equestrian injuries: a review of the literature, a report for the Accident Compensation Corporation', MLIS, 2006.

O'Brien, D. (2016) 'Look before you leap: what are the obstacles to risk calculation in the equestrian sport of eventing?', Animals, vol. 6(2): 13.

Pilianidis, T., Kasabalis, A., Mantzouranis, N. and Mavvidis, A. (2012) 'Start reaction time and performance at the sprint events in the Olympic games', Kinesiology, vol. 44(1), pp. 67–72.

Petridou E, Kedikoglou S, Belechri M, Ntouvelis E, Dessypris N, Trichopoulos D. (2004) 'The mosaic of equestrian-related injuries in Greece', Journal of Trauma, vol. 56(3), pp. 643–647.

Posner, M. and Boise, S. (1971) 'Components of attention', Psychological Review, 78 (5), pp. 391–408.

Ripley, A. (2009) *The Unthinkable: Who Survives When Disaster Strikes—and Why*, Arrow Books, Great Britain, p. xxi.

Rogers, M., Johnson, M., Martinez, K., Mille, M. and Hedman L. (2003) 'Step training improves the speed of voluntary step initiation in aging', The Journal of Gerontology, vol. 58(1), pp. 46–51.

Romano, L. (1995) 'Riding Accident Paralyzes Actor Christopher Reeve', Washington Post, 1 Jun, 1995, p.A01 [http://www.washingtonpost.com/wp-dyn/articles/A99660-1995Jun1.html]. Accessed Jun 2016.

Safe Work Australia. (2014) 'Guide to managing risks when new and inexperienced persons work with horses.' ISBN 978-1-74361-481-5.

Sternberg, S. (1969) 'Memory-scanning: mental processes revealed by reaction-time experiments', American Scientist, vol 57(4), pp. 421–457.

Triantafyllopoulos, I., Panagopoulos, A. and Sapkas, G. (2013) 'Mid-thoracic spinal injuries during horse racing: report of 3 cases and review of causative factors and prevention measurements', Case Reports in Orthopedics, vol. 2013, Article ID 715409, 4 pages.

World Health Organisation. (2000) 'Obesity: preventing and managing the global epidemic,' Report of a WHO Consultation, WHO Technical Report Series 894, Geneva.

INDEX

abdominal exercises, 42, 56, 64, 71
aerial skills, 78, 92, 94
age, 2-3, 14, 19, 21, 53, 62, 154
air-board, 87-88, 94, 106, 112, 117-118
air jackets, 3
amount of training required, 10, 24 154
angry cat position, 60, 66, 142, 144-147
angular momentum, 5, 6, 28, 37, 88
approach run speed/distance, 94, 119
backward candle, 68, 145
backward roll, 12, 33, 69, 74, 84, 122, 145-146, 156
backward fall/landing technique, 33-34, 44, 69
balance, 4, 6, 21, 28, 132
basic jumps, 12, 79-82, 92
basic rolling techniques, 11-12, 69, 83
basics, 4, 10-11, 13, 24, 46, 51, 61-62
benefit of fall safety training, x, 22
bicycle simulation, 44, 130-136, 160
biomechanics, 37
body mass index, 152
body protector/vest, 3, 14, 46, 59, 62, 141, 150
body shape(s), 6-7, 12, 30, 36, 42, 49-50, 57, 60-62, 64, 66-67, 69, 71, 73, 77-78, 88-89, 96, 98, 120, 134, 139, 142-151, 235
brace position, 6, 11, 18, 20, 24, 26, 35-36, 40-41, 49-50, 52, 59-61, 63-66, 58, 70, 88, 125-127, 134, 138
candle position, 68-69, 74
centre of gravity, 15, 86, 155
centrifugal force, 37, 41, 50
Cheales, Barry, vii
choice reaction time, 21
combination activities, 83-85, 88, 90
conditioning exercises, 10-12, 24, 42, 48, 53, 57, 59, 62, 141-150, 152

crashmat, 10, 14, 86, 87, 92-93, 104, 108, 111, 155
crush injury, 3, 30, 32, 36
dive roll, 12-13, 43, 47, 51, 62-63, 75, 98-113, 117, 123, 129-130, 135-136
dress rehearsal, 46
egg roll, 12, 73, 89, 96-97, 156
emergency dismount, 25-27, 31-32, 36, 127, 137, 156
emergency response action, 5-6, 18, 21, 28, 36, 49-51
environmental simulation, 45, 47
equestrian vaulting, 1
equipment for fall safety training, 12, 117
expectancy, reaction time, 18-19, 21-22, 49
fall safety
  instructor, 9-10, 13, 137
  research, 2, 4, 9, 18-19, 152
  technique analysis, 49, 88
  training benefits, 6, 10-11, 22, 47, 49, 53, 163
fall scenarios, 9, 17-18, 21, 28, 48, 50, 117, 137
fall simulation activities, 44, 124, 137
fall times, 5, 15-17, 22
feet-first landing, 11, 25, 29, 38-39, 51, 62, 65, 78, 154
flank vault, 120-122, 128, 156
flexibility exercises, 53-54, 57, 69
flight time, 78, 100, 102, 110, 121, 148, 150
foot position on landing, 118
forces of impact
  landing at speed, 5, 27-30, 34-37, 41, 96, 98
  vertical landing, 16, 29, 32, 35, 37-38, 40, 67
forces of rotation, 37, 41, 50
forward roll, 70-71, 90-93, 95, 115, 119, 125-126, 143-150, 156
forward somersault, 108-116

Index

four-point landing, 16, 29-30, 51, 56, 60-62, 66-67, 70-73, 75, 85
Gladwell, Malcolm, 15, 18
gymnastics training, vii, viii, ix, 1, 5-7, 9, 11, 13, 64
hand position on landing, 66, 105
handstand roll, 12, 66, 76-77, 156
head-first fall/landing direction, 32, 39-40, 47, 50, 98, 130, 134
height of fall, 15, 86
height progression guidelines, 13, 15, 86, 90
high-speed falls, 5, 7, 42, 50, 62, 87-88, 94
history, 1
horizontal momentum/speed, 5-6, 15, 35, 87-88, 107, 109, 130
horse and rider fall scenarios, 9, 17-18, 21, 28, 48, 50, 117, 137
injury prevention, 2, 5, 57
instructor, meaning of qualified, 9-10, 13, 137
intuitive, 4, 13, 20, 24, 28, 36, 41, 45, 49-51, 62, 78
Jander, Caron, vii
joint mobilisation, 54-55
jump half turn, 78, 82, 84, 89-90, 93-94, 106
jumps obstacle, 3, 13, 19, 23, 28, 45, 47-48, 105, 117, 123, 129-130
kinaesthetic awareness, 6, 18, 23, 34, 108, 112, 141
Kovacs, Akos, iii, 163
landing at speed, 5, 27-30, 34-37, 41, 96, 98
landing surface, 14, 47, 62, 83, 85-86, 90, 92-93, 98, 100-101, 103-104, 107, 119, 126, 128, 154-155
latency of response time, 19-20
martial arts training, 6-7, 9, 11
mechanical horse, 4, 9, 43-45
mini-trampoline, 86-87, 92-94, 99, 104-106, 109-110, 112, 114-116, 120-121, 128, 155
movement time, 18, 20
multiple incline roll, 89, 96, 156
muscle conditioning exercises, 43, 45, 53-54, 56-57, 62, 67, 69, 152
muscle memory, vii, 6, 10, 20, 24, 48
myths, 5, 11
neck exercises, 57, 59, 61, 141, 152
neural pathways, 20, 47-48
Newton's first law of motion, 37, 41
Newton's second law of motion, 37
number of training sessions, 10, 24, 154
open tuck position, 57, 64, 68, 81, 98, 108-109, 111, 114, 134
Payne, Michelle, 52
Player, Gary, 53
pre-ride safety routines, 6-7, 11, 24, 48, 54, 57, 59, 61-62, 67, 69, 98, 125, 141-151, 156
pre-ride warm-up, 53-54, 59, 61
prone fall/landing direction, 16, 29, 30, 67, 89, 135
protective clothing, 14, 62, 69, 73, 77-78
qualified instructor, 9-10, 13, 137
quantity of training, 10, 24, 154
reaction time
  and age, 19, 21, 23, 153
  and gender, 19
  choice, 21
  expectancy, 18-19
  test, 153-154, 156
Reeve, Christopher, 52
relaxing in a fall, 6, 41-42, 50-51, 73, 108, 134, 138-139
replica horse, 12, 25, 27, 45, 47, 105, 117, 127-129
research, vii, viii, 2, 4, 9, 18-19, 152
response action in emergency, 5, 6, 18, 21, 28, 36, 49, 50-51
response time
  definition, 18
  effect of training, 20, 22
rock and roll, 46, 59, 68, 70-71, 142, 146
Ripley, Amanda, 22, 117
rolling skills/techniques
  backward, 12, 33, 69, 74, 84, 122, 145-146, 156

rolling skills/techniques (con't)
  forward, 70-71, 90-93, 95, 115, 119, 125-126, 143-150, 156
  sideways egg roll, 2, 73, 89, 96-97, 156
  sideways shoulder roll, 12, 60-61, 67, 69, 72, 85, 91, 95, 122, 143, 145, 147, 149-151, 156
rotational fall, 28, 32, 35, 130
safety belt, 10, 112-114, 133-135, 154
safety considerations for training, 9, 11, 69, 98
sideways fall/landing technique, 30, 67, 137-138
sideways shoulder roll, 12, 60-61, 67, 69, 72, 85, 91, 95, 122, 143, 145, 147, 149-151, 156
simple reaction time, 18-21, 153
simple reaction time test, 153-154, 156
simulation activities, 98, 105, 117, 124-125, 127-139
skill retention, 6, 10, 24, 43, 48, 53, 59, 141
skills assessment, 152-156
skills transfer, 6-7, 20, 43, 45, 47-48, 62, 125, 131
somersaulting, 4, 23, 34, 64, 78, 108-116
spaced repetition, 24, 48
speed progression guidelines, 13, 87-89, 94-97, 106-107, 131-136, 155
spontaneity, 15, 23
spring-board, 87-88, 94
star jump, 54, 80, 84, 91, 93-94, 106, 146, 156
straddle vault, 118-119, 156
straight jump, 54, 78-83, 90, 93-94, 106, 144, 154-156,
theory and science, vii, 10-11, 15-52
time
  available in a fall, 5, 15-17, 22
  to learn fall safety skills, 10, 24, 154
  response time, 18-19, 20-22
trample injury, 28, 36
tuck-and-roll, 5-8, 27, 29-30, 32, 35-37, 41-42, 45, 49, 50, 52, 62, 88

tuck jump, 54, 81, 84, 93-94, 113, 156
unconscious learning, 20, 23-24
unexpected fall, 19-21, 53
vaulting skills, 11, 13, 117-123, 127, 155
vertical impact force, 16, 29, 32, 35, 37-38, 40, 67
vest/body protector, 3, 14, 46, 59, 62, 141, 150
warm-up activities, 10, 12-13, 53-62, 65, 67, 125, 141-150
warning signals, 19, 21-22, 49

ABOUT THE AUTHOR

Lindsay Nylund was born in Western Australia and commenced gymnastics at age eleven. His achievements as a gymnast include three junior and two senior Australian national all-around titles, All-American honours as a member of the Arizona State University Men's Gymnastics Team, and representing Australia at World Championships and Commonwealth and Olympic Games. He won a silver medal in the 1978 Commonwealth Games in Edmonton, Canada, which was the first individual international medal for Australia in gymnastics.

Lindsay's school gymnastics coach in Western Australia was Hungarian-born Physical Education teacher Akos Kovacs. Before immigrating to Australia, Akos was detained as a political prisoner following the Second World War. While being transported by train to a labour camp, Akos decided escape would be a better option than the labour camp. This required jumping from a moving train. Akos gives an account of this incident in the book *Akos Kovacs: an Hungarian–Australian Odyssey*, by David Mason-Jones (1997):

> In all my years at Christ Church Grammar School, I never once told a boy that gymnastics might enable him to jump, handcuffed, from a moving train in a totalitarian state. Nevertheless, let me now state categorically: one of the benefits of good gymnastic training is to enable you to jump, handcuffed, from a moving train in a totalitarian state! Only my gymnastic ability saved me. I tucked instinctively into a ball and tried to roll with the momentum rather than resist. I caught the downward slope of the embankment and rolled end over end for an age before coming to rest.

Following his success as a gymnast, Lindsay coached gymnasts from beginner to international level, including numerous state and national champions in both men's and women's gymnastics. He was appointed head coach of the WA Institute of Sport Men's Gymnastics Program which was recognised as the most successful junior men's gymnastics program in Australia over a number of years. His achievements have been recognised by Gymnastics Australia with an athlete Award of Distinction, an athlete Roll of Honour and a Coach of the Year Award.

Lindsay's qualifications include a Certificate III in Fitness, a Certificate IV in Training and Assessment, a science degree in physical education, and a master's degree in human resource management. Lindsay is committed to reducing injury rates from falls to riders of all disciplines. This book has been written to assist riders, instructors, safety and industry professionals to learn about fall safety training and contribute to improved health and safety for all horse riders.

www.ingramcontent.com/pod-product-compliance
Lightning Source LLC
Chambersburg PA
CBHW070617300426
44113CB00010B/1564